Re-engaging Young People in Education

D1477725

Many young people failed by the school system are those who face a range of social and economic challenges due to multiple forms of injustice. This book provides an insight into the educational practices that work to re-engage young people who have become disenchanted with traditional schooling. It examines the lives of students and workers who participate in education sites on the fringes of mainstream education, and includes a rich tapestry of personal experiences from those who have been failed by their schooling experiences.

The book draws upon research of international relevance conducted in a range of 'flexible learning centres' and 'democratic schools' in Australia and the UK; it suggests that improving the retention levels of young people in formal education will require schooling practices to change. Students who have become disengaged from mainstream schooling do re-engage in the learning process of many alternative schools, indicating that teaching practices and forms of organization which work in alternative sites can also provide lessons for mainstream schooling, thereby encouraging a more socially just education system.

Included in the book:

- contexts of contemporary schooling
- who chooses flexible learning centres and why
- democratic schools: students and teachers working together
- teaching in 'the margins'
- case studies: 'oppositional alternatives'.

All young people have the capacity to learn and to enjoy learning; they do not 'fail school', rather, *schools fail them*. The teachers, workers and students who have shared their stories provide significant insights into how we might change this situation, and the book will be invaluable reading for postgraduates and researchers in the fields of education, the sociology of education, school reform and social work.

Martin Mills is Research Professor in the School of Education at The University of Queensland, Australia.

Glenda McC ool of Education and Professional Studies at G

Re-engaging Young People in Education

Learning from alternative schools

Martin Mills and Glenda McGregor

Routledge
Taylor & Francis Group

LONDON AND NEW YORK

First published 2014
by Routledge
2 Park Square, Milton Park, Abingdon, Oxon OX14 4RN

and by Routledge
711 Third Avenue, New York, NY 10017

Routledge is an imprint of the Taylor & Francis Group, an informa business

© 2014 M. Mills and G. McGregor

British Library Cataloguing in Publication Data
A catalogue record for this book is available from the British Library

Library of Congress Cataloging in Publication Data
Mills, Martin, 1957–
    Re-engaging young people in education : learning from alternative schools/
Martin Mills, Glenda McGregor.
        pages cm
    1. Alternative education—Australia.   2. Alternative education—Great
Britain.   I. McGregor, Glenda.   II. Title.
    LC46.8.A788M55 2013
    371.04—dc23

                                                                        2013017684

ISBN: 978-0-415-50504-8 (hbk)
ISBN: 978-0-415-50505-5 (pbk)
ISBN: 978-1-315-88043-3 (ebk)

Typeset in Galliard
by RefineCatch Limited, Bungay, Suffolk

Printed and bound in Great Britain by
TJ International Ltd, Padstow, Cornwall

Contents

Acknowledgements

We would like to thank our various colleagues at The University of Queensland and Griffith University who provided the space for discussing many of the issues raised in this book. You know who you are. We would like to acknowledge the support we have received through the Australian Research Council (ARC) to undertake aspects of this work. We have also benefited from conversations with Debra Hayes and Kitty te Riele who work with us on a related ARC project. Our friend and colleague, Bob Lingard, has always been a wonderful source of support and enthusiasm. We appreciate this very much. We would also like to thank Youth Affairs Network Queensland (YANQ) and our colleagues on the YANQ Education Policy Advisory group for their support, especially in the early days of this research, but also for their on-going commitment to the rights of young people. Katrina Brink and Ady Boreham have been particularly helpful and supportive at different stages of the research and writing process. Thanks to you both. Thank you Aspa Baroutsis for all the editing and commenting on earlier drafts of this book; we really appreciated your feedback. And Anna Clarkson and Clare Ashworth have been wonderfully patient. Thank you.

We would like to thank our respective children: Glenda – Christopher, Vanessa and Scott who are always in my heart and thoughts.

Martin – Ali and Tara ever patient and tolerant – love always.

We especially want to thank the people, both young and old, in the various schools that we visited. We were received with great generosity and openness. We are extremely appreciative of your trust. Thank you for allowing us into your lives.

The book has drawn on data and arguments earlier presented in McGregor, G. and Mills, M. 2012. Alternative education sites and marginalized young people: 'I wish there were more schools like this one'. *International Journal of Inclusive Education,* 16(8), 843–862 and McGregor, G. and Mills, M. 2012. Teaching in the 'Margins': rekindling a passion for teaching. *British Journal of Sociology of Education.* Available as iFirst DOI: 10.1080/01425692.2012.740813.

Martin would also like to acknowledge his sister, Nicki, who died much too young during the writing of this book. She was not served well by school, but made major contributions to a more socially just society through her participation in peace protests, including at Greenham Common, and work with the squatting movement in Brixton and environmental groups in Australia. She is greatly missed.

List of abbreviations

ABS	Australian Bureau of Statistics
ACT	Australian Capital Territory
AIG	Australian Industry Group
AITSL	Australian Institute for Teaching and School Leadership
COAG	Council of Australian Governments
DEEWR	Department of Education, Employment and Workplace Relations
DfES	Department for Education and Skills
DSF	Dusseldorp Skills Forum
EUDEC	European Democratic Education Community
GCSE	General Certificate of Secondary Education
GERM	Global Educational Reform Movement
ICT	Information and Communication Technology
IDEN	International Democratic Education Network
IEA	International Association for the Evaluation of Educational Achievement
MCEETYA	Ministerial Council on Education, Employment, Training and Youth Affairs
NAIDOC	National Aborigines and Islanders Day Observance Committee
NAPLAN	National Assessment Program – Literacy and Numeracy
NCLB	No Child Left Behind
NGO	Non-governmental Organization
NSW DET	New South Wales Department of Education and Training
OECD	Organisation for Economic Co-operation and Development
Ofsted	Office for Standards in Education, Children's Services and Skills
OP	Overall Position in a state-wide rank order based on the student's academic achievements
PISA	Programme for International Student Assessment
PRU	Pupil Referral Unit
QCT	Queensland College of Teachers
SATs	Standardized Assessment Tests or Statutory Assessment Tests
SES	Socio-economic status
TIMSS	Trends in International Mathematics and Science Study
UCCYPF	Uniting Care Children, Young People and Families

1 Introduction

'Freedom' is a problematic term. There is a Billy Bragg song that we particularly like that points out that a lot of 'liberties' have been taken in the name of 'freedom'. We agree. In the field of education the concept of 'Free Schools' has gained popularity in Sweden, in the United States (known there as 'Charter Schools') and more recently in the UK. Such schools may be set up under the auspices of parents, teachers, charities and businesses. Although they need government approval to operate, and are still subject to inspections, they are 'free' to teach according to whatever model or educational paradigm they have adopted. However, just whose interests are served by this 'freedom' is not always clear and the increasing involvement of entrepreneurs in education is a cause for concern. The notion that market 'freedom' will produce better schools and stronger outcomes for students is an idea that has become popular with many governments; yet the evidence presented in this book, as in others, indicates that such market-driven educational 'freedom' regularly disadvantages some of the most marginalized young people in the Global North. For those young people who may lack the social and economic capital to successfully navigate a competitive society premised on 'freedom of choice', the accumulated consequences may be devastating, leaving them with little capacity to change their circumstances. Yet, in its utterance, the word 'freedom' still captures a powerful sense of calling for a better world, a world where attempts to create a more socially just society are welcomed. Throughout this book the word appears almost forty times, sometimes in our own text and sometimes in the interview transcripts. We critique it when it appears in neo-liberal rhetoric and yet understand its pulling power when articulated by students and teachers who have felt oppressed by structures within, as well as outside, schools. By subscribing to an alternative vision of schooling, one that recognizes that the yearning to be free is best satisfied when aligned with a concern for social justice, we hope that we can give voice to some of the concerns articulated by young people and teachers who have rejected various oppressive structures, ironically constructed in the name of freedom.

This book is partly born out of frustration with mainstream schooling. We are highly committed to a free public education system that caters to the needs of all young people. However, to date, we have seen little evidence that suggests such a system is on the horizon for much of the Global North. There are some exceptions, of course. Some would quite rightly point to the ways in which Finland has transformed its education system into one that is internationally recognized both for its high academic achievements and its commitment to equity (see for example, Sahlberg 2011; Reay 2012). Others would highlight the successes of the early childhood education project in the Italian city of Reggio Emilia (see for example, Fielding and Moss 2011, pp. 3–9) and the Citizen Schools' project in the Brazilian district of Porto Alegre (Gvirtz and Minvielle 2009; Gandin and Apple 2012) as examples of systemic reform. These few cases, however, just exacerbate our frustrations as current trends, specifically in the locations with which we are most familiar, Australia and the United Kingdom (UK), but clearly existing elsewhere, appear to be taking the public education system in a completely different direction. For example, the ways in which an increasing focus on international and national test scores as a marker of a system's or a school's quality working against the interests of the most marginalized students has been well documented (see for example, Lingard 2010; Apple 2010). Further, at the same time as we have seen government schools fearful of losing their competitive edge, we have also witnessed an increasing willingness to remove the 'rubbish' students (to paraphrase Bauman 2004) from schools; to mimic the authoritarianism and trappings of elite private schools; and to focus on a limited set of learnings at the expense of both creativity and student welfare. We have also observed highly committed teachers working in environments where their professional expertise is devalued, where divisions are created between teachers through performance pay debates, and where they feel pressured to be other than the kind of teacher they would like to be (Ball 2003).

Given our commitment to a public education system, it might seem strange that we have gone to schools operating outside of that system for solutions to some of the seemingly intractable social justice challenges plaguing government schools. However, we wanted to find schools that were resisting what Fielding and Moss (2011, p. 136), drawing on Unger (2004), have referred to as 'the dictatorship of no alternative' in order that we could demonstrate the ways in which schooling could be different. We therefore went in search of schools that were 'irregular' (Slee 2011) in the sense that they were not driven by dominant neo-liberal discourses, but rather were underpinned by a stated commitment to social justice. These philosophies recognized the disadvantages that some young people faced because of their material circumstances; the discrimination that some young people faced because of, for example, their gender, race or sexuality; and/or the lack of voice that young people had in mainstream schooling. We hope that in providing examples of such alternatives we can help to challenge the impossibility of constructing a public education system that is shaped by social justice principles.

In addition to frustration, this book is also born out of our admiration for those teachers and workers, whom we came to know via this research, who were operating in highly challenging circumstances with some of the most disenfranchised young people in Australia and the UK, and by the successes that they were having with (re)engaging these people in learning. At the same time we were also impressed by the teachers and workers in schools who were 'living their politics' through a commitment to democratic forms of school governance. But, most of all, we have felt compelled to tell the stories of the young people we have met, who have shared their aspirations for the future and willingly divulged their histories whilst articulating the challenges they have faced in terms of acquiring an education. Many of these young people were not wanted by the mainstream. Thus, one of the purposes of this book is to suggest the ways in which the mainstream can change so that such students feel wanted and listened to in ways that acknowledge the significant challenges that they face outside of school. As such we hope that this book can make a contribution to discussions about creating a public system that is genuinely inclusive and that is comprised of schools that reflect Fielding and Moss's (2011) understanding of 'a radical democratic common school premised not on uniformity but on diversity and plurality' (p. 113).

Thus, this book examines the lives of young people and workers (teachers and youth workers, along with a variety of people from disparate occupational backgrounds) who participate in education sites on the fringes of mainstream education. Found within such fringes are students who are marginalized by poverty and other difficult life circumstances; there are also middle-class students who have the resources to pay for an alternative education. This book provides insights into the educational practices that work to (re)engage young people such as these, who for a variety of reasons, have become disenchanted with traditional schooling practices. Whilst the sites considered in this book cater to a small section of the student population in the UK and Australia, they nonetheless provide salutary lessons for policy regimes concerned with increasing rates of schooling completion. The data presented in this book indicate that achieving this goal will require mainstream schools to change. Evidence from the research points to the need for mainstream schools to support the material needs of students; to provide greater flexibility for students in terms of attendance, learning and assessment modes; and to engage in a re-envisioning of teacher–student relationships, including pedagogical relationships, and democratic modes of governance.

There is growing interest in alternative schooling models as responses to access and equity, and increasing the rates of schooling completion for marginalized young people. For instance, in the United States (US), the Federal Department of Education commissioned a nationwide study of alternative schools (Carver *et al.* 2010), and the John Gardner Center at Stanford University has set up a project on alternative schools in California; in Australia the Victorian and Australian Capital Territory (ACT) governments have both commissioned reports on alternative schooling (KPMG 2009; Mills and McGregor 2013); there is a significant debate in the UK and Sweden about free schools (Bunar 2008; Barker 2010; Leeder and Mabbett 2011; *The Economist* 2011); and a similar interest in alternative schooling models has been evident in Sweden, Germany, the Netherlands and Canada (see for example, Harper *et al.* 2011; also Ontario Ministry of Education 2010). We hope that this book makes a contribution to this burgeoning literature by looking at the ways in which alternative forms of schooling can inform practices in mainstream schools. In particular, we are especially concerned with those practices that offer a deeper understanding of how to create a more socially just education system. Drawing once more on the work of Fielding and Moss (2011) our intent, therefore, is to contribute to a 'hopeful discussion of transformation' (p. 135).

In participating in this discussion we are of the view that in their current form many schools, and the systems in which they are located, create and perpetuate inequalities and oppression. Indeed, at many levels, schools can be regarded as 'violent' (Harber 2004) or 'damaging' institutions (Francis and Mills 2012a). Such harm is brought about through practices that discriminate against the poor and against particular ethnic and racial groups and deny young people a voice in key decisions affecting their welfare. Such harm is both apparent in the present, for example, in relation to harassment and bullying, and in the long term, for instance, in terms of closing down future opportunities. In this book we suggest that the creation of a socially just schooling system would require alternative visions of how schools could work to address these injustices. Such visions, or 'real utopias' as Wright (2010) refers to them, should not be regarded as blueprints that hold 'true' in a range of locations and times. However, as Wright (2010) also argues, 'what can be worked out are the core, organizing principles of alternatives to existing institutions, the principles that would guide the pragmatic trial-and-error task of institution building' (p. 7).

In sketching an alternative vision of schooling from the lessons learnt from the schools in this research project, we draw on the work of feminist philosopher Nancy Fraser (1997, 2010), as have others in the field of education (see for example, Keddie 2012; Power 2012; Blackmore 2013). Fraser claims that there are three forms of injustice: economic, cultural and political. She argues that people experience economic injustice as maldistribution, where a lack of economic security affects a person's life opportunities and futures. Addressing this injustice, she argues, requires a redistribution of resources. Cultural injustice grows out of misrecognition where people's differences are not respected and where those from non-dominant cultures are expected to conform to cultural norms based on factors such as gender, sexuality, ethnicity and class. Addressing this injustice involves recognition and valuing of non-dominant cultures. Fraser argues that political injustice occurs when people experience misrepresentation; that is, when they are denied the opportunity to make justice claims relating to their experiences. Such injustices can be prevented, she suggests, when people have avenues through which to make representation on matters that impact upon them. These three forms of injustice, she recognizes, are not mutually exclusive and at times may conflict with one another. However, they do provide a useful framework for analyzing schooling practices and for engaging in an 'institutional imagination in the spirit of realistic utopianism' (Fraser 2010, p. 44). As we demonstrate throughout the book, and particularly in Chapter 6, the flexible learning schools, in varying degrees, had redistributive processes in place to ensure that students' attendance was not affected by their financial circumstances, and along with the democratic schools had a significant focus on a positive recognition of difference, for example, in relation to gender or race, and/or sought to ensure that students and teachers were able to articulate concerns and shape key policy directions within their schools. Fraser argues that the struggle for social justice in all of these areas is to ensure 'parity of participation' (Fraser 2010). Many of the students we interviewed for this book indicated that their alternative schools enabled them to participate in the education process in a way that had previously been denied them. The barriers that prevented their participation in mainstream schools, for example, poverty, pregnancy, parenthood, cultural discrimination and lack of opportunities to air grievances, were all considered surmountable. As such, we hope that the schools in this study can contribute to a vision of what a socially just school might look like if it were framed via principles of redistribution, recognition and representation.

Research processes

For our project, we avoided schools structured around a particular educational ideology or religion (for example, Montessori, Steiner, Catholic, Islamic etc.) because the nature of the official practices and belief systems in such sites were officially pre-ordained. Further, our intent was to explore what our chosen sites might contribute to a 'school for all'; we concur with Fielding and Moss (2011) who have indicated that it is not the place of such a 'common school' to inculcate a particular set of religious beliefs. We also rejected referral or behaviour-management centres because, rather than offering an 'alternative' pathway, such places are often about 'fixing up' young people to return them to their original school. Pending further evidence, we are also sceptical about the contribution that England's 'free schools' will make to the provision of real alternatives to main-stream schooling options. Although government-funded, these new schools will be unpredictable in terms of their pedagogical practices and curriculum. Under the 2010 Academy Act, parents, charities, religious organizations and commu-nity organizations can apply for approval to set up a 'free school'. They will not be obliged to conform to union agreements nor offer the national curriculum (Cabinet Office 2010). Additionally, there is ample evidence that the concept of English free schools has been derived from the Swedish model that allows compa-nies to own and fund schools for profit (Hatcher 2011). This raises significant questions in respect to the types of schools that might evolve under this system. Indeed, free schools may be more authoritarian and output-focused than current mainstream schools and, depending on the level of unionism in these schools, staff may experience serious vulnerability around conditions and security of employ-ment. Further, claims that the marketization of education, such as in English and Swedish free schools and in similarly structured Charter schools in the US, will contribute to better outcomes have been discounted by Organisation for Economic Co-operation and Development (OECD) research that shows

> It is far from clear that quasi-market forces such as increased autonomy, competition and choice have led to improved outcomes, which would

indicate that educational innovations are occurring. Evidence of improved academic outcomes is mixed, and improvements in academic performance may result from factors other than quasi-market incentive.

(Lubienski 2009, p. 27)

Whilst it may be theoretically possible to set up socially just schools within the free school paradigm, we have yet to see the evidence and therefore have omitted them from our considerations here. In this project we looked for alternative education sites that rejected deficit constructions of young people; and that had certain principles of social justice at their core. As such we were looking for schools that were not simply an alternative to be tolerated and accommodated within existing structures, but were what Raymond Williams (2005) would describe as 'oppositional', in that they could be used to encourage education systems to recognize that in relation to social justice most report cards would read 'could do better'.

In reference to social justice, we looked for principles articulated within the work of Nancy Fraser (1997, 2010) as discussed above. We concur with her standpoint that in determining socially just outcomes we must be sure that people are materially and economically secure; that we 'recognize' – respect – differences of, for example, gender, race, class, ethnicity, sexuality; and ensure that people are able to have political 'representation' and make justice claims on their own behalf – i.e. have a voice. The 'alternative' models of schooling that most closely fitted our intent were what have sometimes been referred to as 'second chance' schools (Ross and Gray 2005; Gallagher 2011) and democratic schools (see Apple and Beane 1999a). In total, ten alternative education sites (six in Australia, four in the UK) were studied in order to explore the ways in which such schools attempted to meet the needs of young people for whom the mainstream schooling sector had become an unattractive option.

Initially we looked at 'flexible learning centres' or 'flexi schools' that were providing young people with 'second-chance education', or in the case of some of the young people we met – third, fourth, fifth, sixth chance education. Students who attended such sites often had challenging life circumstances related to poverty, family mobility, homelessness and early parenthood. Most had experienced significant conflict within previous schooling experiences. The age range of students was broad, ranging from early teens through to early twenties. Many were returning to education after a long absence. The flexible learning sites also provided varying amounts of counselling, assistance with finding accommodation and financial resources, and help with childcare and personal advocacy. They had a strong resemblance to what has been termed 'full-service schools' (Dryfoos 1998; Dyson 2011), or schools that provide 'wraparound' services that respond to the personal, social and economic needs of their students. Most of the young people interviewed who had rejected mainstream schooling were highly engaged with the learning opportunities provided to them at these sites. This engagement appeared to be linked to a combination of factors related to the curricula offered, pedagogical practices and staff relationships with young people, all underpinned by the philosophies shaping each centre's organization.

The democratic processes that we found in the flexible learning centres subsequently led us into exploring the democratic schooling movement, both in Australia and abroad. We made contact with three English democratic schools, including the famous Summerhill[1] (Neill 1970; Stronach and Piper 2009; Lucas 2011), although this school eventually declined to participate in the research due to the ill health of a key staff member. Subsequent visits to all three schools revealed processes of education that echoed those that we had encountered in the Australian flexi schools. Although the democratic movement is not as strong in Australia in secondary education as in Europe and the UK, on our return to Australia we located a high school in a major Australian city in the State of Victoria that shared a similar structure and ethos to those we had visited overseas. Whilst in the UK we also sought out two English flexi schools so that we could compare their experiences and processes with findings at our Australian sites.

Methodology

For this research we decided upon a qualitative methodology based upon interviews and observations. We compiled notes about each site and conducted interviews with a range of students and staff. In the analysis of our data we looked for thematic commonalities and contradictions across texts in order to assemble evidence to support interpretations and conclusions that respond to our overall research question: What are the key features of alternative education sites that work to engage young people in meaningful education and how might such practices inform the mainstream?

This methodological approach was informed by the work of Clandinin (2007), who, along with Connelly (Connelly and Clandinin 1990) proclaims the appropriateness and justice of allowing the narratives of participants to stand on their merit, not as universal 'truths' but as individual experiences upon which we may reflect. Their work draws upon Dewey's (1938) conception of 'life as education' as well as a long history of qualitative methodology involving participant observation, ethnography and narrativity. We suggest that such a research framework is especially appropriate for researching young people, particularly marginalized young people, because it allows people to share their stories, and, to paraphrase Edward Said (1994), 'speak (*their*) truth/s to power', in their own words, metaphors, gaps and silences. It therefore allows the perspectives of the marginalized to be foregrounded.

Initial visits were conducted at each site according to when the schools could accommodate us and lasted for approximately one week. As much as possible we continued to maintain contact with subsequent short-term visits; thus, we do not present complete ethnographic narratives and data, but rather a series of thematic snapshots of participants' experiences of life and educational journeys. Detailed ethnography would have required a more complete immersion in the schools over a much longer period of time. In this project, our purpose was to utilize the experiences of many participants in order to identify thematic commonalities and contradictions across texts that would provide insights into the work of alternative schools. In the analysis and synthesis of data we also included a variety of stages of drafting and cross-checking with participants in order to make sure that we had heard them correctly and that we were representing their experiences with integrity.

Given the relatively small size of the schools and the intimate nature of some of the classes we found we actually had considerable time to observe and interact with the participants. We conducted interviews with a range of students at each site and gathered school documents. Interviews were carried out individually or within the context of focus groups, depending upon the personal preferences of the young people involved. Adult personnel available to be interviewed depended upon the nature of the site and included teachers, workers, parents, volunteers, administrators and social workers. Interviews lasted from 30 to 90 minutes and were electronically recorded and then transcribed. Pseudonyms are used for all sites and participants.

The research schools

The sites (in alphabetical order) from which the data have been collected for this book include:[2]

- Cave Street Flexi School – a non-fee-paying school with one classroom located under a suburban house in a regional Australian city. The school was funded by donations from a group of government schools, and offered a basic year 10 curriculum to approximately 20 young people who had 'dropped out' of school;
- Distincta College – a fee-paying secondary school in a major Australian city that was framed around a philosophy of 'no rules' and was located in a large old house. Along with various other subjects, it offered a traditional academic curriculum from year 8 to year 12. The school had an outstanding academic reputation;
- Ertonia Flexible Learning Centre – a non-fee-paying flexible school that offered General Certificate of Secondary Education (GCSE) courses in core subjects, along with a life skills curricula; it operated across five sites in a large English city. The school supported young high school-aged people in danger of being excluded from school or who did not have access to a mainstream school; most were referred by local high schools. These schools contributed funds to the centre;
- Feldspar School – a small fee-paying secondary school offering core GCSE subjects, located in rural England which operated out of a large house and was designed around a Summerhill philosophy of democratic education. It catered to students whose families were concerned about what they perceived to be oppressive practices in mainstream schools;

- Fernvale Education Centre – a non-fee-paying, church-supported school, located in a suburban area of a large Australian city. The school offered a standard curriculum to girls, many of whom had experienced difficult personal circumstances or had had their education at other schools interrupted by pregnancy and childbirth;
- St Ebenezer School – a large school catering to students from pre-school to senior that was located in a UK satellite city. It had a history grounded in the principles of Quaker education, although did not see itself as a 'Quaker school'. It described itself as 'multi-faith/no faith' and offered a vegetarian lunch so as to be inclusive of all beliefs. The school had high fees, catered to students who did not conform to mainstream expectations and prided itself on its academic record;
- The Garage – a non-fee-paying 'workshop' school that was housed in a large industrial shed in suburban Australia and provided young people who were failing to attend school with opportunities to acquire a year 10 qualification and workplace certificates, the latter primarily related to motor mechanics. The school was funded by a large charitable organization;
- Victoria Meadows Flexi School – a non-fee-paying inner city Australian school supported by a local council and a Catholic educational organization. The school had originated in a park but at the time of our visits operated from the premises of an old school, catering to a diversity of students, many of whom were homeless and faced severe social problems;
- West Canal Alternative School – a non-fee-paying alternative school, located in an old library building in a regional English town. The school offered vocational and core GCSE subjects to young people who had struggled to fit into and succeed in mainstream schools; and
- Woodlands Flexi School – a non-fee-paying rural flexi school in regional Australia run under the auspices of a local, large high school that tended to support students from a white, working-class, rural community. It provided a range of individualized educational pathways that included year 10 and workplace certificates and the possibility of continuing on to a local university.

For a variety of reasons, many of the young people who attended these schools had become alienated from schooling processes at an early age. They came from a diversity of social backgrounds. Some came from privileged circumstances, but had experienced conflict with teachers due to their unwillingness to conform to the authority structures of mainstream schools, or they had suffered social isolation because of their lack of conformity, for example, to normalized gender constructions, and had therefore chosen an alternative educational pathway. These students were often found within the fee-paying democratic schools. However, in the non-fee-paying alternative sites visited, large numbers of students came from working-class backgrounds and racial and cultural minorities. Many of these students faced major social issues including homelessness, lack of family support networks, financial problems and drug dependency, sometimes along with carer responsibilities for their own children, siblings or other family members. Often suspended from, excluded from or simply by refusing to attend their mainstream schools, these young people now accessed their education from sites purposively created to provide alternative, *positive* schooling experiences.

During the course of the research we discovered that it was not only the young people in the case study sites who had felt marginalized within mainstream schools. Also marginalized were many of the teachers now working in these alternative schools. This was particularly so for those teachers who demonstrated a strong commitment to democratic pedagogies and holistic education as opposed to the more instrumentalist educational framework currently favoured by neoliberal educational authorities. However, the staff in some of these schools were often working in conditions that saw them underpaid in relation to their colleagues in other settings. Conditions often depended upon whether schools charged fees and whether they had access to various types of government and community support. There were also additional emotional demands placed upon many of these teachers as they faced the ongoing problem of connecting with young people who had been alienated by and were consequently distrustful of adult-run systems of education. Yet, despite such challenges, teachers and other workers seemed extraordinarily committed to the task of re-engaging young people in an education that was meaningful to the young people and facilitated their aspirations for the future. The reward for teachers and workers alike was quite simple but hugely meaningful: job satisfaction – they loved their work, had professional freedom and felt they were making a real difference to the lives of their students.

A note on terminology

This research has occurred across two English-speaking locations which have slightly different terms. When writing about sites we have used the local terminology, for example using 'principal' when writing about Australia and 'headteacher' when writing about the UK. Similarly, at times, we use the term 'school retention', not to describe the practice of making students repeat a year of school, but to refer to schooling completion, usually to senior levels. There were also some terms that were contentious in our research sites and in various public presentations we have completed. These terms included 'mainstream' and 'alternative'.

It was argued by some, for instance, that the term 'mainstream' homogenized systemic schools, denying the ways in which some government schools have demonstrated a significant commitment to addressing various social injustices. We do recognize that such schools and their teachers exist and that they too can present a challenge to conventional practices (see for example, Munns *et al.* 2013). However, the majority of such schools are also located within a systemic framework that is, as we argue in Chapter 2, problematic. Furthermore, to date we have not come across many systemic schools that provide the types of support available within many of the flexible learning centres represented in this book. We do acknowledge that some 'full-service schools' (Dryfoos 1998;

Dyson 2011) are moving in that direction; although, again, many of these sites are still structured along hierarchical lines with the young people attending them having very little representation in the making of key decisions. We would also note that when we are referring to 'mainstream' we include the vast majority of private schools within this definition. Additionally, it is necessary to point out that some of the alternative sites in our study were run by systemic schools. In attempting to address some of these critiques we considered other terms such as 'traditional' to describe what the schools in this book are not. However, many of these terms also have their own definitional problems. For example, 'traditional' has overtones of rigidity and fixity. We believe that such a term does not capture the state of contemporary schooling. As such we have stuck with the term 'mainstream' throughout the book, but acknowledge the inherent problems in using it.

'Alternative' was also critiqued by some people in the sites we visited on the grounds that it suggested that they were not 'real schools' and hence were not providing a 'real education' (see Chapter 5, p. 93). We understand the problem with the term. However, we have been concerned that apart from the types of schools we have worked with for this book there are few opportunities for young people who have been alienated within and by their experiences of schooling to take up other options. This dearth of alternatives has posed a problem for many young people. Therefore, we want to highlight that there are other ways for schooling to be. We also note that we were not simply looking for 'alternative' schools, but as indicated above, also 'oppositional' schools. However, it is our hope that one day we will not need such terms to describe schools, preferring, like Kitty te Riele (2012), that there will just be a variety of equally valid and equally valued 'learning choices'.

In discussing the work that has occurred in the group of sites that we have referred to in this book as flexible learning centres, the term 'school' has also been problematic for us. All of the sites represented in this book were either a registered school or were an off-site centre run by a school. Many of the sites required school registration in order to obtain funding. However, some took on the name 'school' grudgingly, and only for funding purposes. In such cases it was argued to us that 'school' represented something that many of the young people attending the site had been trying to avoid because at some stage it had let them down. For many of these people they wanted their 'learning centre' to be seen as a welcoming place for those who had been disenfranchised by the mainstream education system and suggested that their attempts to build community along non-hierarchical lines was not captured by the term 'school'. There were also people who did not like the phrase 'second-chance education' as, they indicated, it implied that the young people were being given a second chance due to their own failures, not that they had been denied the right to an education in the first place. We are sympathetic to this view, but at the same time we recognize that these young people have indeed been given a second chance by the actions of those who work in the flexible learning centres. We also draw upon the growing body of literature that uses the term second-chance school (as noted earlier, examples include Ross and Gray 2005; Gallagher 2011). In the main, we have referred to this type of site as a flexible learning centre; however, at times do include the term school where a particular site had it in its title. Thus, names will vary depending upon the preferences of a particular site.

The term 'democratic' was also problematic for us because of its contested meanings (see Chapters 4 and 6). Some people emphasize its political intent, whilst others foreground it as having a symbiotic relationship with social justice. Addressing this tension has proved difficult when writing about the 'democratic schools' in our study, especially given we align with the latter view. The democratic schools that we have focused on in this book were all fee-paying, which of course has social justice limitations, but they also had a system of organization that worked to ensure that young people and teachers had a say in the governance of their own school. We have thus referred to these schools as democratic, and as we indicate in Chapters 4 and 6, some of these schools also attempted to act in 'oppositional' ways.

We therefore ask our readers to consider the complexity inherent in all the terminology we have used in describing our research sites. Indeed, we hope that this book will incite further discussion about other currently popular schooling terms such as 'accountability', 'efficiency', 'knowledge economy', 'performance indicators' and 'teaching and learning audits', to name but a few. Through this book we aim to contribute to a growing counter-narrative to such neo-liberal, managerialist discourses, suggesting a new framework of terms that describes what schools might be, could be and should be. In his study of the relationship between language and power, Fairclough (1989) notes that 'consciousness is the first step towards emancipation' (p. 1). We are confident that the voices of the young people and those of the teachers and workers in alternative schooling sites presented in this text will contribute significantly towards raising such consciousness.

Organization of the book

Chapter 2 of the book explores key issues in respect to the international policy context and national political debates in respect to school completion and youth welfare. Such debates are contextualized within a broad analysis of social, economic and cultural factors, including gender, race, ethnicity and class, all of which are significant shapers of schooling success. We also consider the nature of many mainstream schools and how particular schooling practices may impact upon young people, their learning and their sense of belonging to their school.

Chapter 3 focuses on flexible learning centres, and examines the educational histories of some of the students who attend them; it explicates reasons for their (re)engagement in learning and outlines their aspirations and plans for the future. What is clear from these sites is that their success was in large part due to their responses to the material and welfare needs of the students. Why young people stayed was also important. The quality of the curriculum and pedagogy, the flexibility of staff and the school and the relationships between staff and students were integral to the reasons why many of these young people attended school on a regular basis.

Chapter 4 is concerned with some of the implications of the governance processes found in a set of 'democratic' schools. The schools we looked at here were all fee-paying, although some of the practices found in them were present in some of the flexible learning centres. Whilst we are concerned about the accessibility of these schools to some young people, our focus in this chapter is on what can be achieved when young people are given a voice. The benefits of this student-centred approach to schooling included young people's sense of the following: ownership of the school; responsibility for themselves and others; self-confidence and worth; and a commitment to the principles of active citizenship. However, this approach was not without issue in respect to the impact upon other aspects of day-to-day running of the schools. Pathways through some of these tensions are considered in this chapter.

Chapter 5 focuses on the workers and teachers we met at each set of sites. Here we explore their motivations and teaching philosophies; their frustrations and success stories. We investigate why they continued to work in these sites for less money, often in poorer working conditions; and we explore the kinds of professional (and other) support that they thought necessary for themselves along with promoting the long-term existence of the sites. We also present their perspectives on the aspects of alternative schooling that worked and those that needed improvement within their sites. Underpinning this chapter is the notion of 'emotional labour' and its cost to the teachers and workers who staffed these sites. At the same time there are lessons in this chapter about the types of conditions that need to exist in order for teachers to realize many of the reasons which first attracted them to teaching.

Chapter 6 brings together many of the lessons from the previous three chapters to explore the ways in which these schools address economic, cultural and political injustices. Drawing on Fraser's (1997, 2010) understanding of social justice, we provide three cases studies (two flexible learning centres and one democratic school) to foreground the ways in which injustice can be challenged within schooling contexts. We are not holding up any of these schools as an ideal school; instead, we seek to demonstrate that there are real alternatives to the ways in which most mainstream schools operate; and that such ways have the potential to address many of the inequities currently being perpetuated within those schools. As such we would make the distinction here, as do Woods and Woods (2009c, p. 228), drawing on Raymond Williams (2005), between 'alternative' and 'oppositional'. We suggest that the schools presented in this chapter are not just alternative but also oppositional in that they represent, in varying degrees, a challenge to the traditional grammar of schooling (Tyack and Tobin, 1994).

Chapter 7 sums up our data and the conclusions we have drawn in respect to alternative schooling. Here we present our concluding arguments about the significance of alternative education sites and the need for greater systemic support for and recognition of the role that they play in catering to the needs of many young people. However, we also consider some of the social justice implications of moves towards greater numbers of alternative flexi-type schools catering to students from low socio-economic backgrounds. Similarly we are concerned that the benefits of the democratic principles and practices found in some alternative schools are only accessible to middle-class students. Thus we conclude with some of the implications our research has for the mainstream sector.

Notes

1 A. S. Neill's Summerhill School, a co-educational boarding school in Suffolk, England, is the original alternative 'free' school. Founded in 1921, it continues to be an influential model for progressive, democratic education around the world.
2 See the Appendix for more detail about the schools.

2 Contexts of contemporary schooling

This chapter explores key elements of the policy and political landscape within which schools are currently trying to serve the interests of their students. Here, we also consider some of the key social, cultural and economic factors that are highly influential in shaping schooling success. The rise of alternative education, in its many forms, has fuelled debates about the currently dominant paradigm that seems to favour a 'corporate' model of schooling based upon 'inputs', 'outcomes', 'accountability regimes' and frequent use of standardized tests to 'measure' the educational progress of their 'clients'/students. As education budgets come under pressure, governments across the world have allowed increasing corporate sponsorship of schools in order to provide basic educational materials; the application of business models to school leadership in schools is also common practice (Douglass Horford 2010). In the US, Sweden and Canada 'Charter Schools/Free Schools' that have greater autonomy within the public systems are sometimes entirely sponsored by corporations; this system has been criticized for making it easier for corporations to 'educate for the market' (see for example, Bjorklund *et al.* 2005; Beder *et al.* 2009). As noted in the Introduction to this book, in seeking our research sites we were not interested in such 'alternative' models of schooling as these because they seem to echo and even enhance dominant mainstream schooling practices and beliefs; nor did we look to schools that were shaped by particular religions, ideologies or deficit constructions of youth. We sought alternative sites that might provide fresh insights into schooling practices that were grounded in principles of social justice; as such, they stood in opposition to many historically entrenched beliefs about the nature and purpose of mass education. Here, it is necessary to consider such ideas in order to understand just what our selected alternative sites were rejecting.

The inherited traditions and practices of systems of mass education were shaped during the rise of industrial societies and fashioned to provide levels of education needed to facilitate the growth of capitalist systems of mass production. Prior to the modern era a comprehensive education was only accessible to the wealthy, powerful and privileged classes, within which males were further privileged in respect to accessing types of learning related to public careers. However, with the rise of industrialization and the modern nation state came a range of skills required by citizens and workers and subsequently the need for mass schooling. Thus, during the nineteenth century, the social, economic and industrial conditions of rising nation states in the Global North facilitated policies that would see the eventual extension of education to all. It has also been suggested that these changes were linked to the desires of some governments to direct and control the ideas and attitudes of their populations. Indeed, Green (1990) argues that the provision of mass schooling in countries such as the US and those of the UK and Europe was *mostly* about controlling the masses: 'The task of public schooling was not so much to develop new skills for the industrial sector as to inculcate habits of conformity, discipline and morality that would counter the widespread problems of social disorder' (p. 59).

The totalitarian regimes of the mid-twentieth century provide numerous examples of the use of education for the purposes of state propaganda and inculcation of particular attitudes. However, even the most apparently benign democracies engage in the socialization of the child into the mores of the time and place in which they are born and raised. Tensions continue today as to the balance between education for the sake of the individual versus education for the good of the state and its economic interests. However, whilst noting the ongoing debates about the most appropriate curriculum for particular times and places, it is evident that on the whole, the *structures* of mass schooling have remained fairly constant. In the main, it continues to be highly institutionalized, hierarchical and controlled either by governments or, in the case of private schools, by wealthy elites or religious bureaucracies. Harber (2004) argues that the authoritarian nature of traditional mass schooling tacitly supports an ethos of violence against youth. He cites the perceived *right* of schooling institutions to punish young people in a variety of ways which until recently, in most developed countries, included acts of physical violence. His view is supported by Ross-Epp (1996), who argues that:

> Systemic violence begins with the expectation that all students of similar ages should and can learn the same things. Children are placed with large groups of similarly aged students and teachers are forced to adopt methods of control and routine that would be better left to the military, the workforce or the penal system . . . In a quest for conformity, students are monitored in their coming and going, they are required to carry hall passes and must seek permission to leave the room. Their activities are directed, and timed, and their learning is scheduled into periods of work followed by short breaks. Such regimentation requires rules and punishment and administrative models that rely on differentiated power relations.
>
> (Ross-Epp 1996, p. 17)

Drawing upon the theory of Michel Foucault, one might, therefore, view schools in the same light as other 'disciplining' institutions. Foucault asks, 'Is it surprising that prisons resemble factories, schools, barracks, hospitals, which all resemble prisons?' (Foucault 1977a, p. 227). In an interview with Gilles Deleuze, Foucault continues to highlight the authoritarian nature of schools:

> If the protests of children were heard in kindergarten, if their questions were attended to, it would be enough to explode the entire educational system . . . Not only are prisoners treated like children, but children are treated like prisoners. Children are submitted to an infantilization that is alien to them.
>
> (Foucault 1977b, pp. 209–210)

Surely then it is not surprising that within traditional mass schooling, many contemporary young people begin to resist the disciplining practices that are part of the authoritarian heritage of such institutions. Indeed, it sometimes appears that while secular, pluralist societies have become more open to choice and difference, schools have increased the regimes of surveillance and control of their students. Consider the differences in respect to the rights and freedoms of senior high-school students and first-year university students. Many of these young people are exactly the same age, yet the ways in which they are expected to behave towards adult authority are markedly different.

Moral panics around perceptions of 'unruly youth' have a long history and continue to attract significant media coverage (Osgerby 2004). Political responses have routinely favoured a punitive approach; for example, from October 2010, school principals in Queensland were granted increased powers to suspend and/or expel students. Since then there has been a steady increase in the number of suspensions and expulsions. According to published data from Education Queensland, reported in the media:

> Exclusions from individual schools have surged by 50 per cent, from 766 cases in 2006–07 to 1176 last financial year [2011–2012] . . . The spike comes after principals were given the power to directly expel students without departmental permission.
>
> (Fraser and Chilcott 2013, p. 1)

In 2011, out of a total population of just under 500,000 primary and secondary students in Queensland there were 62,000 suspensions (Chilcott and MacDonald 2012). Of these, it is alleged that 20,000 suspensions were for violent behaviour. Additionally, 1,000 students were permanently excluded. This story made front page news in the local paper as well as being widely reported online. To exemplify the situation, journalists referred to several extreme cases of student violence that included stabbings. Moreover, a deconstruction of the text reveals the use of emotive language that demonizes the young people in the stories; they were described as 'outlaws'; 'dangerous'; 'violent'; and 'disruptive'. However, such reporting simply serves to skew public concern towards a minority of cases and draw attention away from the 40,000 young people who were suspended for such reasons as 'disobedience, misconduct and other conduct of the student that is prejudicial to the good order and management of the school' (Education Queensland 2012). Interestingly, Education Queensland has recently adopted a new term for suspensions and expulsions; they are now 'disciplinary absences'. We suggest that this change serves to emphasize that it is the child who is entirely at fault and in need of such 'disciplinary' measures. The greater licence to interpret and punish behaviour such as 'disobedience' (for example) that principals now have, has placed students at risk of being suspended for reasons that have little to do with violence, as is evident in the following data:

Reasons for the 1–5 day suspensions in Queensland in the four terms in 2010–2011 were:

- 32.3% for physical misconduct
- 23.1% for verbal or non-verbal misconduct
- 14.9% for other conduct prejudicial to the good order and management of the school
- 9.4% for persistently disruptive behaviour adversely affecting others
- 6.9% for refusal to participate in the programmes of instruction
- 6.4% for property misconduct
- 4.6% for substance misconduct involving tobacco and other legal substances
- 2.1% for absences, and
- 0.3% for substance misconduct involving an illicit substance.

> (Strategic Policy and Research Program, Commission for
> Children and Young People and Child Guardian 2012, p. 77)

What is interesting is that approximately 55 per cent of short suspensions were for 'offences' not injurious to others or their property. Moreover, it seems bizarre that 2.1 per cent of students were suspended for absenteeism! As the Queensland *Snapshot 2012* demonstrates, the breakdown for longer suspensions is similar:

> The main reasons for long suspensions were physical misconduct (34.3 per cent), other conduct prejudicial to the good order and management of the school (18.6 per cent), verbal or non-verbal misconduct (18.5 per cent) and persistently disruptive behaviour adversely affecting others (8.1 per cent). Over one third (37.3 per cent) of exclusions were the result of physical misconduct; one fifth (19.9 per cent) for other conduct prejudicial to the good order and management of the school; 17.9 per cent due to substance misconduct involving an illicit substance; and 9.7 per cent for verbal or non-verbal misconduct. All cancellations were due to students' refusal to participate in the programme of instruction.
>
> (Strategic Policy and Research Program, Commission for
> Children and Young People and Child Guardian 2012, p. 78)

The fact that one's enrolment may be cancelled due to a lack of participation indicates a very weak systemic response to the problems of those students whose circumstances inhibit their capacity to comply with schooling demands. Additionally, the numbers may be skewed towards the suspension and expulsion of students in minority groups. In the Australian State of New South Wales (NSW), for example, Aboriginal and Torres Strait Islander young people make up just 6.1 per cent (Office of Public Schools, Department of Education and Training (NSW) 2013) of the NSW school population, but 23 per cent of all long suspensions (Research and Program Development, Social Justice Unit, UCCYPF 2011; see also Graham 2012).

This apparent 'war' between segments of the student population and school authorities suggests a number of social, economic and educative problems that need to be addressed. Rarely, however, does the media spotlight interrogate the very nature of schooling that continues to assume the subordination of the young as appropriate. Indeed, certain young people are constructed as 'the problem', and 'the solution' is to suspend or exclude them from schooling institutions. The representation of youth in stereotypical binaries of good/bad, co-operative/wild, moderate/promiscuous or earnest/lazy has been common media-speak since the 'creation' of the 'teenager' in the 1940s (Osgerby 2004). Consequently, it is all too easy for adults to demand a return to a more stringent 'disciplinary gaze' (Foucault 1977a) that becomes part of a 'governing metaphor' (Yeatman 1994, p. 112) of saving/protecting the 'good' youth from the 'bad'. Such attitudes may be taken up by public figures seeking simple solutions in the face of overwhelming social and cultural complexity instead of the more complex task of addressing the inequalities that underpin such tensions in schools.

Traditionally, young people have been regarded as 'empty vessels' that could be filled with the expertise and information required by industry (Boli *et al.* 1985). The hierarchical governance still favoured by most mainstream schools continues to mirror the management of industrial factories. For several decades now, educational researchers have stridently critiqued this paradigm of schooling and predicted its demise, as evident in Allan Luke's observation:

> Traditional classroom notions of schooling based on thirty desk-based kids with all eyes up front on the teacher will not be the model of schooling and learning in the near future. The single-file movement of students from class to class, from subject-area to subject-area, is a product of industrial model schooling, an out-dated disciplinary regime both in terms of disciplining students and in accessing the disciplines.
>
> (Luke 2003, p. 81)

The research of Luke and others (see for example, Newmann and Associates 1996; Hayes *et al.* 2006) indicates that best practice in areas of pedagogy and curriculum is reflected in classrooms that are student-centred, collaborative, intellectually challenging and supportive. However, along with outdated notions of mass schooling, there is also a new paradigm of education that contributes to undermining such models of child-centred learning. The goal of 'human capital' production (Andreas 2009) is currently one of the prime drivers of national education policies. Opposition to processes of a 'marketization' of mainstream schooling figured strongly in the foundation of the types of alternative schools that fuelled our interest in this research. It is to such influences that we now turn.

Educating for 'prosperity'

Prior to becoming Prime Minister of Australia after the 2007 election, Kevin Rudd launched his ideas for an 'education revolution' that looked beyond *social* investment in schooling, stating 'there is now incontrovertible evidence that education should be understood as an *economic* investment' (Coorey 2007, p. 1, emphasis added). He went on to make clear links between school retention and the future economic prosperity of the country:

> Australia spends well below the Organisation for Economic Co-operation and Development average on early childhood education and has one of the lowest retention records for secondary school students . . . Our investment in human capital is essential for creating an innovative, productive workforce that can adapt to a rapidly changing world. We must embrace a new national vision – for Australia to become the most educated country, the most skilled economy and the best trained workforce.
>
> (Coorey 2007, p. 1)

We see similar sentiments in the following excerpt from British Prime Minister David Cameron's speech about education reform:

> Yes, we're ambitious. But today, we've got to be. We've got to be ambitious if we want to compete in the world. When China is going through an educational renaissance, when India is churning out science graduates . . . any complacency now would be fatal for our prosperity.
>
> (Cameron 2011)

This political focus upon the economic good that flows from an educated populace is detrimental to the individual and social benefits of education. Indeed, in the face of what Pasi Sahlberg (2011) refers to as the *Global Education Reform Movement* (GERM) it is becoming increasingly difficult to mount counter-narratives to the economic imperatives of schooling. Elements of the instrumentalist trend underpinning GERM include the following: a narrowing of curricular choices; exam-based accountability measures for students; performativity requirements for teachers; a de-professionalizing of educators via the increased prescription of pedagogical templates and workbooks; and a preoccupation with literacy and numeracy, all contextualized within discourses of parental choice and the marketization of education (Apple 2007; Sahlberg 2011).

Contemporary education policies are thus formulated at a national level within volatile contexts of integrating economies; economic, environmental and military crises; and the increasing mobility of people either by choice or circumstance

(Bauman 1998). Despite the global financial crisis early in the new millennium, in nations of the Global North the neo-liberal paradigm continues to influence the thinking of state leaders, particularly in respect to education policies which continue to follow business models based upon numerical 'measures', standardization, accountability, consumer 'choice' and the individualization of success and failure. According to Apple:

> Neoliberal, neoconservative and managerial impulses can be found throughout the world, cutting across both geographical boundaries and even economic systems . . . Policies are 'borrowed' and 'travel' across borders in such a way that these . . . impulses are extended . . . and alternative or oppositional forms are marginalized or attacked.
>
> (2010, p. 2)

Both within and among nations, due to historically entrenched 'asymmetrics of power' (Lingard 2007), the effects of such impulses upon education are uneven and produce differential benefits to the privileged and the marginalized populations in specific locales. In nations of the Global North, this marginalization is linked to issues such as poverty, race, ethnicity and gender in complex combinations with each other and many other individual factors of 'difference', for example, various learning disabilities and mental health issues. However, there is also a marginalization of *ideas*. The rhetoric of 'freedom', as associated by the political Right with deregulation of the market place and small government, has come to dominate official conceptions of schooling, recasting parents and students as 'consumers' and students as 'human capital' (Apple 2007). Ironically, such (neo)'liberal' agendas often serve to suppress the professional freedom of many teachers. For instance, the surveillance of teachers' work via the collection of data about their performance and that of their students enables the creation of a bureaucratic 'panopticon' (Foucault 1977a) producing 'a kind of data madness' (Kuehn 2005, p. 47) that facilitates processes of de-skilling teaching professionals.

Situated within the eye of this educational storm are the students, some of whom are amongst the most marginalized in their respective societies. It is this latter group of students who, for many complex reasons, often struggle to complete their schooling. In the public domain, the outputs of education systems have become so inextricably linked to national economic prosperity that opposing views about the nature and purposes of education have been silenced and/or marginalized. This 'economization of education policy' (Lingard 2009, p. 81) has evolved via neo-liberal policy frameworks that privilege theories of 'human capital' production (Ball 2006), performativity (Lyotard 1984) and standardized testing. Within this new 'moral economy' (Ball 2006) of individualism, a form of educational Darwinian ethos prevails as self-interested 'consumers' and 'clients' compete for the spoils of the schooling 'marketplace' shaped by a national and international competitiveness that fails to address the impact on student performance of socio-economic and cultural differences. Rizvi and Lingard (2010) argue that the global context within which educational policy is conceptualized means that solutions to national/local educational injustices must also be globally situated. Thus it is necessary to explore the educational terrain as it appears on a global scale.

The global educational environment

Increasingly, during the last thirty years, national educational authorities have become subject to the competitive pressures of international testing regimes. These include the OECD measure of student achievement, the Programme for International Student Assessment (PISA) and Trends in International Mathematics and Science Study (TIMSS) sponsored by the International Association for the Evaluation of Educational Achievement (IEA). Within the Global North, the effects of being a part of the global education market include the roll out of national curricula (for example, Scotland's *Curriculum for Excellence* and the *Australian Curriculum*); the establishment of literacy and numeracy standards; national tests (for example, SATs[1] (Standard Assessment Tests) in the UK for years 2, 6 and 9 and Australia's National Assessment Program – Literacy and Numeracy[2] (NAPLAN) for years 3, 5, 7 and 9); the establishment of school inspections (for example, the UK's Ofsted, Office for Standards in Education); and the rise of teachers' accreditation bodies that prescribe standards that have to be met by teachers in order to gain registration. For example, in 2006 the Queensland College of Teachers (QCT) in Australia introduced 195 such standards (Queensland College of Teachers 2006) that attempted to describe the minutiae of what teachers must be able to know, practice and value. As we go to print, in Australia plans are well underway for the introduction of a comparable regime of national teaching standards.

In the UK, the two agencies that were responsible for the regulation of the teaching profession, the Training and Development Agency for Schools and the General Teaching Council of England were replaced by the Teaching Agency in 2012. Thus, increasingly, teaching has become state business and educational 'outputs' have become measurements of national competitive advantage. As Lingard (2011) argues, 'Numbers, categories, data, statistics are central to this technology, are central to achieving cybernetic input-output equations demanded by the contemporary neoliberal state' (p. 365). Such a technocratic business model is likely to conflict with the 'emotional labour' (Hochschild 1983) inherent in teachers' work, and, as noted by Ball (2003), leads to 'a struggle over the teacher's soul' as well as diminishing the joy of learning for many young people. As indicated by Wisehart (2004, p. 46), 'When we reduce learning in our students' eyes to numbers and letters, we lose passion, we lose complexity, we lose fun, we lose depth, we lose the essence of learning.' What 'counts' as important knowledge is currently defined in quantitative ways thereby potentially limiting the possibilities for engaging students in personally meaningful modes of learning (McGregor 2009). We therefore contend that the work of teachers has become increasingly about meeting systemic demands of accountability, leaving less time for their core business of teaching. Darling-Hammond (2004) points to the narrowing of the curriculum, the focus upon teaching-to-the-test and emphasis upon lower order thinking skills that are the consequences of the 'accountability systems' of the neo-liberal, globally powerful educational discourses serving to shape national educational policies. According to Raider-Roth (2005), such a policy context de-professionalizes many headteachers and teachers by its deficit of trust:

> As a society, we no longer trust principals to make curricular decisions for their schools . . . We no longer trust teachers to make curricular and classroom decisions . . . the aggressive proliferation of standardized testing similarly communicates our profound distrust of teachers' ability to teach . . . Most disturbingly, we are losing trust in children's drive to learn, as is evidenced by the implementation of high-stakes testing . . . which suggests that unless children are threatened with dire consequences of failing . . . they will not learn.
>
> (2005, p. 17)

We suggest that educational social justice is difficult to achieve within this 'panopticon' of state distrust of those who work closely with the individual circumstances of the socially alienated and disadvantaged young. Such is the nexus at which globally shaped education policies, premised upon perfor-mativity, accountability and prescriptive curricula, conflict with best practice in the classroom, and, as indicated by many of the teachers in Chapter 5, make the work of teachers less professionally satisfying. Constrained by state demands to conform to macro-policies of measurement and accountability, the professional identity and actions of the individual teacher may become delimited and hence, potentially, less able to respond to the needs of young people.

Research indicates that disengagement from, and non-completion of, formal schooling is usually the consequence of a complex mix of factors (Smyth 2004; Smyth and Hattam 2004; te Riele 2006; Savelsberg and Martin-Giles 2008; White and Wyn 2008; Taylor 2009; Mosen-Lowe *et al.* 2009). Key influences include social, cultural and economic factors: low socio-economic status (SES); family relationships; gender; language and cultural barriers; racial background; poor achievement; and the desire/pressure to earn money. For the most vulnerable young people these elements are exacerbated by a host of school-related issues that are seemingly oblivious to the personally challenging circumstances of their lives. Additionally, Smyth and Fasoli (2007) argue that research indicates that the problem of disengagement is far more widespread than the number of actual 'drop-outs' may indicate. Disengagement is an insidious process of disconnection from school and the people and processes within it. It signifies a lack of meaningful learning and a relational vacuum that some students simply endure because they have the resources outside of school to compensate, or have the resources, as many of the young people in Chapter 4 had, to choose an alternative form of private education. However, it is the young people whose 'habitus' (Bourdieu 1984), often formed within a context of disadvantage and social dislocation, positions them in conflict with conventional schooling who are most at risk of school disengagement and 'dropping out' (see Chapter 3). Bardsley (2007) suggests that as such students are most vulnerable to the vicissitudes of a global neo-liberal economy, it is imperative that national governments formulate educational policies that ensure that access to an 'effective' education is a *right*, not a privilege. Whilst acknowledging the contested nature of an 'effective education', Bardsley's (2007) argument rests upon the stark correlation between socio-economic background and schooling failure and non-completion. We agree that if governments are to respond competently to these challenges they must address the social and economic elements of the lives of young people.

Social and economic factors

The nature of education systems varies greatly across nations. When examining issues of school completion we are referring to the attainment of upper secondary education or the final stage of secondary education in most OECD countries. According to the OECD (2011), approximately 82 per cent of young people in OECD countries complete upper secondary education, whilst in the G20 nations (a forum for co-operation and consultation on international financial matters) the rate is 75 per cent. This report also identifies, on average, a 14 per cent correlation between the socio-economic backgrounds of young people and their subsequent academic performance at school, although there are variations among countries. Data on reading outcomes from Canada, Finland, Korea and Shanghai, China (for example) demonstrate a lower correlation between background and student achievement (OECD 2011). Race and ethnicity continue to impact upon attainment levels within all SES groups. In France and New Zealand, for example, young people from an immigrant background were an average twenty-seven points lower on levels of reading than young people from a similar socio-economic background (OECD 2011). In England, despite government rhetoric about the need to address attainment gaps between rich and poor (see DfE 2010), social inequalities continue to be reproduced by the education system (Dyson 2011; Equality and Human Rights Commission 2010; Schools Analysis and Research Division 2009). In the US, attempts to address the inequities produced by class and race led to the *No Child Left Behind* (NCLB) legislation (US Department of Education 2001) that sought to respond to poor performances on PISA and TIMSS (West and Peterson 2003). Unfortunately, responses in many countries have relied on market-driven solutions that favour more accountability and high-stakes testing (Finland being an obvious exception to this, see Sahlberg 2011). According to Smith (2010), such measures are 'unproven systems [that] can do much to reinforce inequities and label many otherwise good schools as failing' (p. 38). It would seem that to date, many governments have struggled to address the complex social interactions of class, gender and race that challenge the efforts of schools to raise educational attainment among marginalized populations.

According to the Australian Bureau of Statistics (ABS), in Australia approximately 78 per cent of young people attain year 12 (Australian Bureau of Statistics 2011). However, there is a considerable gender gap with 73 per cent of boys as opposed to 83 per cent of girls completing senior schooling (ABS 2011). The ABS (2011) identifies boys and Indigenous youth (particularly Indigenous boys) as making up a large proportion of the 22 per cent of students in Australia who do not complete year 12. Once poverty is factored in, the dimensions of social exclusion expose an intricate web of interdependent features that work against school completion of the marginalized. Research consistently supports the link between non-completion and low SES (Lamb *et al.* 2004; Ross and Gray 2005; Savelsberg and Martin-Giles 2008; White and Wyn 2008). Moreover, data provided by the OECD indicate that the relationship between socio-economic background and educational outcomes is stronger in Australia than in many other comparable countries (OECD 2011). These factors are magnified by geographical isolation and regional differences indicated by school completion rates of 59 per cent in the Northern Territory compared to 86 per cent in the Australian Capital Territory (ABS 2011). Within the low SES segment of the population, Indigenous students struggle with the multiple challenges posed by geo-location, colonization, and generational marginalization as well as cultural and language barriers (The Prime Minister's Office 2009). Only around 37 per cent of young Indigenous people complete their senior schooling or vocational equivalent (ABS 2011). Many of these problems are shared by refugee and newly arrived immigrant youth. For marginalized young males within all these social categories, the risk of dropping out of school is even greater, although care is needed not to use these data to identify boys as the 'victims' of contemporary educational policies and structures (Lingard *et al.* 2009). Whilst it is true that on the whole completion rates are generally higher for females, research shows that gender continues to be a factor for vulnerable young women from low SES and marginalized racial and ethnic backgrounds, particularly when coupled with teenage pregnancy (Connell 2009).

Families in economic difficulty may also have higher levels of residential and school mobility that impact upon the ability of students to maintain continuity in their academic studies and establish strong networks of support amongst peers. Combined with increased responsibilities in respect to siblings and early job-seeking, such contexts increase the risk of non-completion of schooling (Gray and Beresford 2002; White and Wyn 2008). Research in this area identifies a range of sociocultural disadvantages experienced by some young people right from their first year at school (see for example, Alexander *et al.* 2001). Some students' lack of expertise in a whole range of taken-for-granted middle-class sociocultural situations, or 'cultural capital' (Bourdieu 1984), creates an achievement gap that widens over time unless there is sensitive and sustained intervention by the school (Apple and Buras 2006). If this gap remains and grows the consequences include low achievement, low self-esteem and eventually disengagement from learning (Teese and Polesel 2003), often provoking resistant behaviours in the classroom and school. These challenging behaviours position such students for cycles of conflict with schooling authorities often leading to absenteeism, suspension, expulsion or, finally, dropping out of school altogether.

A generation ago, many young people, particularly from low SES backgrounds, routinely left school early to seek employment. However, rapid sociocultural change and global economic restructurings have made this pathway less viable and fraught with individualized risks. According to respected sociologist Ulrich Beck, society is now characterized by new, unequally distributed risks and challenges that require individual responses:

> Like wealth, risks adhere to the class pattern, only inversely: wealth accumulates at the top, risks at the bottom. To that extent, risks seem to strengthen, not abolish, the class society. Poverty attracts an unfortunate abundance of risks. By contrast, the wealthy (in income, power or education) can purchase safety and freedom from risk.
>
> (Beck 1992, p. 35)

For those young people who are most vulnerable to non-completion, this wider social context adds to their dilemmas. In an era of neo-liberal national educational competitiveness (Apple 2006; Ball 2006) they become 'the problem' for failing to negotiate the hazards of this so-called 'risk society' that demands increasing levels of social, emotional and educational capital to succeed. Schools are positioned to play a vital role in helping students to develop such competencies, but educational authorities must pay greater attention to the broader socio-economic contexts within which these institutions operate. It seems that inherent social inequalities have been downplayed by a resurgent neo-liberal discourse of individual responsibility. Indeed, concepts of 'social justice' have been replaced by particularized forms of 'equity'. Equality of opportunity has overtaken notions of affirmative action along with deficit labels attached to those young people who 'fail' to seize it. An 'equitable' approach ignores the social reality that children start school from very unequal positions which perpetuate class based inequality. Taylor and Singh make this very point:

> [While] . . . shifts in language are not in themselves enough to effect more fundamental changes in approach which are necessary in implementing major educational reforms . . . they may easily result in . . . issues slipping off agendas . . . [and] . . . the particular needs of these groups . . . [being] . . . glossed over, and economic and cultural differences become recontextualised as individual differences.
>
> (Taylor and Singh 2005, p. 11)

Thus, once they enrol some young people struggle to connect with the culture of the school. Their unique background combinations of gendered influences, family practices and support systems, language development, emotional and social capital and class positioning all contribute to the shaping of a young person's attitude towards schooling. Empathy and support systems from the school are therefore vitally necessary to the academic success and social well-being of 1 students. The next section looks more closely at the systemic and school-b: issues that may contribute to early school leaving.

Schooling factors

We argue that a neo-liberal, 'social efficiency' (Bardsley 2007) paradigm of schooling that aims to produce human capital via accountability mechanisms of prescribed curricula and high-stakes testing, is in conflict with the establishment of socially just schools. Such policies produce school cultures premised on a type of individualistic competitiveness that privileges those young people with the greatest social, economic and cultural capital. Within the context of the classroom, these policies translate into processes of increased marginalization of many young people made vulnerable to non-completion of schooling through a variety of factors already cited, that include race, gender and low SES, to name but three. On a school level, headteachers, principals and managers must subscribe to the marketing demands of the corporate presentation of documents, personnel and students in response to the need to attract the 'consumer'/parent. Discourses of discipline, efficiency, success and respectability shape school policies and programmes and subsequently the image of the school. Personal careers and school funding (whether government and/or private) depend upon it. However, the operational imperatives of these aspects of school cultures, and the rules that shape them, are frequently at odds with the needs of vulnerable students.

Rules that apply to uniforms, self-presentation, social interactions and assumptions of unquestioning obedience to adult power, position certain students for ongoing systemic conflict. The young people who live in unstable and/or unsupportive/neglectful environments frequently find it difficult to comply with many of the cultural expectations of mainstream, middle-class schools. Others may struggle with school rules for a variety of reasons that range from behaviours associated with special needs to sophisticated personal philosophies of individual freedom (McGregor 2009). However, we contend that it must never be forgotten that regardless of the reasons, young people (including many young *children*) who are suspended or excluded from school due to behavioural issues, still have a *right* to an education. Research carried out in the UK (Thomson and Russell 2009) argues that school cultures, curricula and practices are all implicated in student disengagement and behaviour and therefore educational authorities have a duty to ensure that all children have access to a high-quality education. It is ludicrous for those holding executive positions in educational bureaucracies to claim, as did the Deputy Director-General of Education Queensland, that students who are excluded from schools can continue their education via distance modes of learning (Fraser and Chilcott 2013). This presumes levels of resources and educational competence that may well be lacking in the home contexts of most of the students who are suspended and/or expelled. If there are some young people who are too 'dangerous' for schools, surely throwing them on to the streets will only exacerbate the problem for them and society at large.

Teachers provide a bridge between young people and education systems, and classrooms are the educational interface at which connection or disconnection occurs for students. Thus the relationships, pedagogical and assessment practices within these classroom spaces are fundamental to engaging and retaining the interest and trust of students (McFadden and Munns 2002; Smyth and Hattam 2004). However, as young people move through primary into secondary schooling and in particular into the senior phase, curricular content and assessment practices become increasingly rigid. The credentialing and rank-ordering of students demand regimes of comparability and uniformity of assessment that take little account of the life circumstances of marginalized young people. Whilst there are sometimes opportunities for students to apply for 'special consideration' regarding the completion of assessment, for example, the reasons are usually limited to fairly specific emergent medical and family circumstances that do not recognize the accumulative nature of the debilitating effects of poverty, family breakdown or conflict, along with the general uncertainty ('risks') of life circumstances that may arise from these and other factors of social marginalization. Additionally, vulnerable students may not have the confidence and/or skills to use systemic avenues of appeal, particularly if they have a history of conflict with school authorities. The system presents itself as an unfriendly maze of rules and paperwork that is overwhelming to students who are often already disengaged and/or alienated from schooling processes. In such circumstances, young people become the problem that needs 'fixing'. Founded on notions of developmental psychology, deficit models of youth frame many responses to non-completion of schooling and educational failure is often attributed to faults within the individual child (Ball 2004). In an age of increasing individualization of risk, the response has been to situate the blame within the student. Quinn *et al.* (2006) argue strongly against this notion, claiming that 'when a child fails to learn and grow, the fault lies not solely with the child but instead lies mainly with the system and the adults responsible for it' (p. 11). te Riele (2007) also makes the point that rather than targeting so called 'at risk' youth – which as Wishart *et al.* (2006, p. 297) suggest is a 'radicalized and classed code' – schools need to change from a focus on uniformity to a focus on diversity.

Official labels such as 'at-risk' and 'disengaged' youth thus tend to individualize the issue of early school leaving, drawing attention away from the contextual issues of teacher–student relationships, curricular content and teaching and assessment strategies. Many classrooms continue to be formal, hierarchical and structured around the accepted power of the teacher to control the content, pace and direction of lessons (McFadden and Munns 2002; McGregor 2009). Whilst most students will endure, though not necessarily enjoy, this situation, for students whose lives have little resonance with the explicit and 'hidden' curriculum of their classroom and who lack the cultural capital necessary to avoid confrontation, disengagement and disaffection with learning are likely, and often understandable consequences. Gable *et al.* (2006) identify a mismatch between the structure of traditionally organized schools and marginalized segments of the population and a failure on the part of such schools to address diversity and a possible school readiness gap. The lack of space for students to insert their own experiences may alienate them from the shared culture of the classroom. Traditional teaching practices that fail to take into account what students bring to the pedagogical relationship risk overlooking many of the underlying reasons for resistant behaviour. Subsequent power struggles between such students and their teachers may lead to increasing levels of coercion and punishments (Gable *et al.* 2006) that erode positive elements of teaching and learning. Thus there is a need for what Smyth and Fasoli (2007) describe as a 'fundamental reworking of schools such that they have a focus on a *pedagogy of relations*' (p. 277, emphasis added); that is to say, quality teacher/student relationships that are at the heart of quality education.

Schools are also often the sites where students give vent to emotions generated elsewhere, such as at home or in social situations with peers (McFadden and Munns 2002). Research into schooling responses to youth crime (Reid 2009) highlights the importance of the role played by teachers in investing relational or emotional capital in their students. Earlier research confirms this perspective, situating emotional capital at the very heart of education. According to Harding and Pribram (2004), 'emotions . . . [have a place] . . . in the production of knowledge, culture, individual and collective identities, and power relations' (p. 864). Emotions experienced by students such as despair, resentment and low self-esteem lead to early school leaving, and, according to Gable *et al.* (2006), 60 per cent of early leavers suffer various emotional problems. On the other hand, the emotions expressed by school authorities often demonstrate simply a desire to rid themselves of the problem. Schools often want such students removed from the school, as illustrated in this comment by a principal interviewed by Skiba and Peterson (2000) who stated that, 'You don't get it . . . we don't want to understand these kids; we want to get them out' (p. 340). Whilst we do not suggest that such a comment is representative of all principals in all schools, it does indicate the complexity and emotionally charged nature of the problem (see also Morrison and Skiba 2001).

Approaches that attempt to 'fix' the student in isolation from contextual influences will continue to falter because they look at only one part of the problem. Reid (2009) suggests that schools can do much more to harness emotion for social benefit. She describes it as 'a socio-cultural product rather than something that resides in the individual psychological make-up of a student' (p. 2). Reid further argues that a lack of hope can lead to disengagement and cites instances of teachers 'investing emotional capital . . . (of engaging) in a form of emotional labour that attempts to induce appropriate behaviour through investing more emotion in a relationship developed through trust' (p. 11). She concludes with a call for schools to facilitate 'networks of trust'. Sidorkin supports this argument by claiming that we must 'restore the power of relations in schools' (2002, p. 80). Whilst it is evident that education providers alone cannot fix the broader socio-economic and cultural influences on the lives of their students, they are positioned to shape learning: learning environments; learning programmes; and the learning that comes from effective teaching, in order to facilitate the well-being and achievements of *all* students – including those from the margins of society.

Unfortunately, the current rates of schooling non-completion that continue to concern governments of the Global North suggest that there are many young people who do not thrive in mainstream schools.

Increasing school completion and alternative education

Government concerns in respect to school completion are evident in many nations of the Global North. For example, in Scotland which, of the four countries in the UK, has the highest rate of young people 'not in education, employment or training' (Evans *et al.* 2009, p. 11; see also Riddell 2009; Finlay *et al.* 2010), there is a raft of policy frameworks seeking to improve that country's retention of students in meaningful education or employment. These policies include *Closing the opportunity gap – anti-poverty framework* (Scottish Government 2008) and *More choices, more chances: A strategy to reduce the proportion of young people not in education, employment or training in Scotland* (Scottish Executive 2006). The policy commitment to young people disengaged from schooling has also been evident in England. For instance, the Department for Children, Schools and Families' *Raising expectations: Staying in education and training post-16* (DfES 2007) is seeking to reduce the number of young people not in education, employment or training in that country. These concerns with re-engagement and school completion in the UK have also led to a number of commissioned research projects into alternative forms of education there. These include, for instance, Barnado's *Second chances: Re-engaging young people in education and training* (Evans *et al.* 2009) and the Rowntree Foundation's *Mapping the alternatives to permanent exclusion* (Thomson and Russell 2007).

In Australia, the so-called 'earning or learning' agenda which began in 1998 progressively recast a universal unemployment scheme as one that is age-specific; in order to obtain the subsequent Commonwealth Youth Allowance, young people aged 16–24 have to be in some form of education or training in order to claim the benefit; or, if aged 16–21, engaged in activities that will lead to employment. Young people who are unable or unwilling to re-engage in mainstream schools must find an *alternative* education/training site before they are able to claim social welfare. This focus on school retention has continued in further government strategies such as the National Partnership on Youth Attainment and Transitions established in 2009 by the Council of Australian Governments (COAG) with the goal of 90 per cent retention by 2015 (COAG 2009). Governments claim that such measures are intended to improve the employment prospects and overall life chances of young people, however, some researchers think otherwise. Wyn and Woodman (2006), for example, argue that moves to increase school retention rates in Australia stem *explicitly* from economic concerns and that such measures are designed 'to coerce young people into remaining in education and training and to limit the proportion of young people who are eligible for government income support' (p. 505).

In outlining targets for improved school completion rates, there has seldom been a focus on changing the ways in which schools operate in order to make them more friendly to those young people who have not fared well at school. In the same vein as Foucault, referenced earlier in this chapter, Teese and Polesel (2003, p. 137) note how 'prison' as a metaphor for schooling is regularly employed by young people who are doing 'poorly' at school. This metaphor is used by both boys and girls. For many of these students then, extending the amount of time that they are compelled to stay at school is tantamount to an extended sentence. Furthermore, if these students continue to receive little benefit for schooling through improved academic outcomes then the justification for these students staying on longer at school is questionable. However, at the same time it is clear that those young people who do not finish school struggle to make progress in the job market. As advanced industrial societies embrace the technological revolution that is removing the necessity of manual forms of labour, the credentialing that allows entry into middle-class 'white collar' occupations is vital. Thus, schools have to address the ways in which their very structures deny access to their benefits to significant proportions of low SES young people. According to Entwistle (2012), schools are essentially middle-class institutions and therefore geared to serving the interests of the children from that class. Therefore we contend that correlations between school completion and later success in life need to be re-examined through the lens of class.

Additionally, there seems to be a tension here between the apparently increasing suspension/expulsion rates of students and school retention. A recent study by Hemphill *et al.* (2010) demonstrates a clear relationship between SES levels and rates of school suspensions. They point out that while such data are not predictive, they indicate that as a rule as community disadvantage increases, so does the likelihood of student suspensions. They point to the pressure felt by mainstream schools:

> Schools located in low SES communities are often stretched by the number of students whose educational progress is influenced by the burden of adversity and social problems that they bring to school. In such circumstances, schools may resort to counterproductive 'get tough' policies to maintain control.
>
> (Hemphill *et al.* 2010, p. 16)

Here it is pertinent to consider, also, the marketization of education and subsequent competitive 'league tables' evident in, for example, Australia's *My School* website. Within the neo-liberal state, schools are forced to compete for students and such data do influence parental choice and funding. Hence, 'troublesome' students who are seen as potentially damaging to the reputation of the school or to the position of the school on various league tables may find that they are encouraged to go elsewhere.

For some young people, the hierarchical relationships between students and teachers, symbolized by the use of titles to address teachers and lack of opportunity for students to challenge decisions made by teachers, are factors that may lead to conflict in the form of 'disobedience' and subsequent suspension. The grammar of schooling has changed very little in response to changes in the demographics of senior schooling and the rules about attendance, uniforms, assignment submission and the right to be treated with respect, for example, have proved very resilient to change. Such patterns of schooling tensions are common throughout the Global North. Many of these students have sought out or been encouraged to find alternative programmes that keep them in education and often on school rolls whilst freeing them from the sources of conflict present in their schools. This in turn has had market implications for the provision of such services. In England for example, there has been a proliferation of alternative programmes being offered to schools there. These programmes are often designed to keep students who are disillusioned with school busy and engaged. There has also been a growth in what has been referred to as 'second-chance schooling' (see for example, Gallagher 2011).

This education sector has also been growing strongly in Australia and as such has come under some scrutiny from various governments. For instance, the Victorian government commissioned KPMG to develop a framework for the provision of different forms of education for disengaged young people (KPMG 2009) and the Australian Capital Territory government commissioned us to undertake research into alternative forms of schooling in that territory (Mills and McGregor 2013). Likewise, our research for this book has been focused on why it is that many young people who have left or been forced to leave mainstream schooling have turned to an alternative education site, often with a much more positive engagement with learning than they had in their mainstream school. Indeed as we will indicate in the next chapter, many of the students in these schools, as with the school students in te Riele (2011) and Hayes (2012), would not be in education if it was not for the existence of a second-chance school.

A note on the middle class

A primary concern of ours in this chapter has been with those young people who experience various oppressive practices because of their socio-economic status, often linked to their racial or ethnic backgrounds. These students' experiences of schooling are the focus of Chapter 3. However, this is not to say that students from more privileged backgrounds do not experience schooling as oppressive. Many young people from a variety of class backgrounds find the lack of opportunity to challenge injustices, to question authority or to make positive contributions to key decisions affecting the student population to be at best frustrating and at times intolerable. Likewise inflexibility, strict uniform guidelines, a focus on test results and school cultures premised on the subordination of young people can feel stifling for *all* students. This is borne out by comments made by the young people whose perspectives on schooling practices inform Chapter 4, Democratic schools. What is different for middle-class students is that if they can manage to tolerate the situation in school, the rewards are likely to be greater for them than for those from poorer backgrounds. Furthermore, for the more affluent sections of the middle class, if they have parents or carers who are sympathetic to their children's plight at school, there are often alternatives to the mainstream that may be easily accessed.

Conclusion

In this chapter we have foregrounded a range of external factors that impact upon successful school completion. Schools exist within a 'glocal' slipstream of educational ideologies and policies. Currently, those that are dominant favour an instrumentalist view of education with measurable outcomes and standards that may be held up for comparison, nationally and internationally. Within the global market, high academic outcomes for young people are routinely linked to high-performing national economies. Young people are viewed as key players – as 'human capital' – in the success of their homelands. In order to 'grow' this resource, educational authorities of the Global North focus upon regimes of instruction that encourage young people to mirror the competitiveness of neo-liberal capitalism. So pervasive is this educational paradigm that other visions of what education could, or should, be are silenced or deemed to be 'alternative'. 'Real education' is equated with what the mainstream has to offer.

Here we have argued that many young people struggle with traditional schooling structures due to a complex mix of social, cultural and economic factors. Due to the increased pressure of systemic demands for accountability and performativity, teachers are challenged in respect to responding to the needs of marginalized and vulnerable young people. Many classrooms have become constrained by the lines of accountability and one-dimensional measurement of student achievement. Valuable teaching time is devoted to preparation for a range of tests that, at best, provide a point-in-time assessment of very base-level skills and rote-learning of 'facts'. Teacher–student mentoring and significant amounts of time are required for more complex tasks that draw upon higher-order thinking processes of analysis, evaluation and synthesis, application and creativity. Within such contexts of meaningful learning, teachers are much better placed to provide the kinds of emotional support and individualized pedagogy required to address the needs of all students, but in particular those who are socially marginalized and/or disaffected with the structures of schools. For this research project we looked for education providers who refused to subscribe to educational instrumentalism; providers who offered an alternative and/or oppositional (see Introduction) model to demonstrate how schools could become more socially just.

Schooling retention rates across the Global North indicate that, at best, around 18 per cent of young people do not finish senior secondary schooling; however the results are skewed because of the higher completion rates in northern Europe. Thus, there are millions of young people who are not accorded their right to a meaningful education. Such numbers indicate that the neo-liberal paradigm, when applied to education, exacerbates already existing social, economic and cultural inequities. Via the perspectives of the young people and the teachers and other school workers who participated in our research, in the following chapters we present alternative ways of viewing and enacting the education of young people within the context of more socially just schooling practices.

Notes

1　SATs are tests given at the end of year 2, year 6 and year 9. They are used to show a child's progress compared with other children born around the same time.
2　National Assessment Program – Literacy and Numeracy (NAPLAN). Every year, all students in years 3, 5, 7 and 9 are assessed on the same days using national tests in reading, writing, language conventions (spelling, grammar and punctuation) and numeracy.

3 Who chooses flexible learning centres and why

Globally, there are many different forms of alternative education sites. They range in intent from behaviour correctional units, through vocationally oriented literacy and numeracy providers to democratic institutions founded upon philosophical beliefs in the rights of the child (Raywid 1994; te Riele 2007; Woods and Woods 2009a). The degree to which Charter/Free schools offer genuine alternatives to the mainstream is subject to some debate, as noted in Chapter 2. Thus, in seeking our research sites, we looked for schools that offered a viable alternative to mainstream practices and could also make a contribution to a conversation about social justice and schooling by rejecting deficit views of the young people who attended them; and developed strategies that catered to the educational, social and emotional needs of the students. Fundamental to this perspective was the notion that there must be educational diversity offered within the context of respect for, and care of, young people. Our research took us to a variety of sites, some of which were funded by the state, some largely funded by parents and others that were dependent upon charitable organizations for their existence. Funding arrangements were clearly significant in terms of the extent to which alternative sites are sustainable in the longer term.

In Chapter 4 we discuss the implications of alternative education accessed through parental choice shaped by social and economic capital. In this chapter, we focus upon alternative education sites variously known as 'second-chance' schools, 'learning choice programmes' or 'flexible learning' centres (see Introduction and te Riele 2012 for a discussion of terminology). Such places offer a 'second chance' to young people who often live in unstable environments and have a variety of life issues that have led to them dropping out or being expelled from mainstream schools. However, as te Riele (2007), who prefers the term 'learning choices', has noted, second chance should not be seen as 'second best' but as a valid educational choice. For consistency of terminology, we are choosing to refer to these sites as 'flexible learning centres' as we see the flexibility present in such sites as standing in stark contrast to the organization of mainstream schooling. Indeed, in one of the sites we visited for this research that was a registered school, the co-ordinator did not want it to be thought of as a 'bloody school', as he claimed that this created a false sense of its mission (see Chapter 5).

ı a number of countries, alternative education sites have become a significant
er in the support offered to young people who have been rejected, or felt
rejected, by mainstream schooling systems. For example, a major survey conducted in Australia in 2011 for the Dusseldorp Skills Forum (te Riele 2012),
Learning choices, identified over 400 programmes, operating at over 1,200 locations, supporting 33,000 young people. The report on this survey also noted
that there were 4,100 young people on the waiting lists for these programmes.
It was suggested in this report that due to the difficulty of locating many sites,
this 'scan' of alternative education provision was likely to be an underestimation
of the actual number of such centres and the students attending them. *Learning
choices* provides an outline of the characteristics of these flexible learning centres.
For example, each site tended to cater to small groups of young people; many
had funding problems; most offered accredited curriculum options; the majority
worked against deficit views of young people; they sought to create an environment that suited the students rather than attempting to 'fix up' the young
person; and most employed a diversity of staff (e.g. teachers, youth workers
and counsellors).

In the UK, as in Australia, there has been an increased demand for alternative
education. According to one government white paper, *Back on track* (Department
for Children, Schools and Families 2008), at least 47,000 young people were in
alternative forms of education at the time, although perhaps this too might be
a severe underestimation as, it has been claimed, 'the true number is at present
unknown' (Ogg and Kaill 2010, p. 14). Again like Australia, there appears to
be a lack of co-ordinated English data that provide information on what programmes and sites exist, what they offer, how many young people are in them
and how they found their way into these learning environments (te Riele 2007;
Thomson and Russell 2009). In England, alternative education provision is
largely seen to include schools, programmes and sites where students who have
been suspended or excluded from mainstream schools are compelled to attend,
for example Pupil Referral Units (PRUs). In relation to our research, these were
not the type of school that we were looking for as we were concerned that the
rationale behind such units tends to pathologize young people's behaviour
without taking contextual factors into account. The primary purpose of most
behavioural sites is 'fixing up' the young person and, along with some other alternative providers, can also be used to get rid of students who are deemed to be a
problem for mainstream schools and teachers. We were also of the same
view as Gallagher (2011, p. 456), who notes in his overview of the Loughshore
Education Resource Centre in Belfast that the success of second-chance schools
is often a factor of attendance being voluntary. Therefore, in our selection of
sites for this chapter, we looked for places where the students (and in some cases
their carers) had chosen their flexible learning centre.

As we indicated in the previous chapter, the increased demand for alternative
forms of education has had a number of policy drivers. Significant here have
been attempts to increase school retention through raising the school leaving
age (te Riele 2007; Evans *et al.* 2009). Ironically, so too have school exclusion

policies, albeit in different ways. In the state in which the Australian sch this chapter are located, government school principals have recently been greater powers to expel students than they had before. This, as noted earlier, led to a spike in the number of students suspended and expelled in Queenslan as demonstrated in newspaper stories such as 'Classroom smackdown' which details a 50 per cent increase in Queensland government school suspensions handed out by principals in the last five years (Fraser and Chilcott 2013). In England there were calls by the new Labour government in the late 1990s to reduce the number of exclusions from schools (Parsons 1999). The strategic way in which some headteachers have gone about this also appears to have had some impact upon the increased demand for alternative education provision (Ogg and Kaill 2010).

In a report by the UK 'think tank' Civitas, *A new secret garden? Alternative provision, exclusion and children's rights*, Ogg and Kaill (2010) point to the way in which alternative education providers are taking on the responsibility of educating those young people not wanted by schools. They suggest that through a referral process to an alternative provider, whereby schools do not exclude students, but keep them on their rolls and are thus still deemed to have responsibility for the young person, schools are effectively hiding their exclusion figures. They consequently argue that 'political pressure to reduce permanent exclusions has led to the growth of new forms of "effective exclusion"' (2010, p. 3). In another report, *Improving alternative provision* (Taylor 2012), conducted for the UK government, the Government's Expert Advisor on Behaviour, Charlie Taylor, is also critical of the ways in which some schools avoid taking responsibility for the young people they are excluding and of their failure to determine the quality of the programmes to which they are sending such students. This is a concern shared by Thomson and Russell (2007, 2009) in the UK, who in their study of alternative education provision in the English Midlands suggest that there are serious issues in respect to the consistency of curricular and pedagogical quality across all of their case-study sites (see also Kilpatrick *et al.* 2007 in relation to these issues in Northern Ireland).

We too are concerned with the way in which alternative forms of education can be used to deny young people a quality education; we also agree that there are quality-control issues related to alternative programmes that need to be addressed in order for such sites to be considered valid alternatives. However, there are many such places that have served to engage young people, who have been failed by the mainstream, in meaningful learning. As such we suggest that these sites do have some valuable insights in respect to supporting and engaging very marginalized young people; these perceptions are worth sharing with the mainstream.

In this chapter we explore the reasons why some of the young people in our study left mainstream schools and how they found their way in to a flexible education centre. In doing so, we situate the experiences of these students within the broader educational policy context described in Chapter 2 which, we argue, currently works against the needs of young people who may be marginalized by their class, race, gender and/or complex combinations of these and other sociocultural and personal factors of 'difference'. As also noted in Chapter 2, many of the young people who are most at risk of non-completion of schooling frequently come from marginalized segments of the population. The personal stresses stemming from poverty, poor health, insecure housing, school mobility and for some, abuse, social isolation and learning and language difficulties, have severe consequences for the continuity and progression of learning. Within the context of mainstream schools young people who experience such challenges often struggle to get the help they need because of the size of classes along with a general lack of *targeted* pastoral care and the wraparound social services required to respond to their individualized life circumstances and possible trauma. Typically, such students either drop out or are suspended/expelled depending on whether their response to their situation is one of passive depression or active rebellion. Students may simply 'disappear' from the rolls unless schools and education systems have efficient tracking mechanisms and the will to re-engage them. Frequently, however, the response from educational authorities seems to be quite the opposite, one of *assisting* schooling authorities in removing so-called 'unruly' youth.

The culture of blame that surrounds 'misbehaving' students is reflected in the headline of an article on school suspensions in the State of Queensland where the Australian flexible learning centres are located: 'Queensland state school suspended 320 rogue students a day in 2010'. The article notes the record breaking level of suspensions (62,800) and expulsions (931) for that year (Helbig 2011). The newspaper also reported on the support principals received from the (then) Education Minister for their tough stand:

> Education Minister Cameron Dick yesterday praised principals for taking a hard line against bad behaviour, saying students who faced disciplinary action should 'have a good hard look at themselves'.
>
> (Helbig 2011)

Whilst individual schools often treat the departure of 'problem' students as a success, policy frameworks recognize that this might not be a positive social or economic outcome for a country. In Australia, for example, The National Partnership on Youth Attainment and Transitions (COAG 2009) is seeking to lift year 12 retention rates from 78 per cent to 90 per cent by 2015 and to ensure that all young people under the age of twenty-five are entitled to an education or training place, subject to course requirements and availability. Underpinning this government resolve is recognition that of students from low socio-economic backgrounds in Australia, only 59 per cent finish year 12 (Gillard 2009). In an effort to lift educational attainment rates in Australia, the government introduced its 'earning or learning' legislation requiring young people to be in education or training in order to qualify for a government funded 'youth allowance' (Department of Education, Employment and Workplace Relations 2009). Consequently, those young people who leave school early are forced to seek alternative forms of education if they are unable to secure employment. Research shows that early school leavers are typically thirteen to fifteen years of age (Thomson and Russell 2007; Mills and McGregor 2010) and are therefore without the formal qualifications that are necessary for the workforce, with many lacking basic skills in literacy and numeracy. Others are battling homelessness, abuse, mental illness and various addictions. Consequently, the aforementioned 'earning or learning' agenda in Australia has forced many vulnerable young people to seek alternative forms of education in order to survive. The demand for places in flexible learning centres in Australia is rising along with increased numbers on waiting lists. According to a major government-commissioned study of school disengagement in the Australian State of Victoria:

> There is currently limited data to quantify the number of children and young people accessing alternative settings. However, anecdotal reports from stakeholders suggest that the educational options catering to children and young people at risk of disengaging or disengaged from school, are experiencing increasing demand. Stakeholders particularly noted:
>
> - increasing numbers of children and young people who are failing to thrive in school settings or are being excluded;
> - capacity issues in some regions due either to the lack of alternative options or waiting lists;
> - gaps in the educational continuum in some regions, with children and young people having to travel significant distances to access programmes (particularly in rural regions);
> - difficulties (within some regions) in accessing services that cater for children in primary schools. There is also difficulty in identifying and obtaining sufficient information regarding the availability and suitability of programmes.
>
> (KPMG 2009, p. 47)

Such findings are supported by our research.

In the UK, investigations into attendance records reveal that there are many students who leave or who are excluded from mainstream schools and remain unaccounted for. According to the OECD (2011), in the UK, there are more young people aged 14–19 years of age not in work, education or training than in other developed nations. OECD (2011) data also rank the UK twenty-sixth out of thirty-five countries, for the number of teenagers who have attained an upper secondary qualification. In England, where two of our flexible learning centres are located, legislation was passed to raise education participation ages to 17 by 2013 and to 18 by 2015 (Department for Education UK 2013). This move is underpinned by the provision of diplomas, vocational and academic pathways, with flexible routing:

> The Diploma provides an introduction to a sector or subject area through a blend of applied and theoretical learning. The teaching and learning focuses on skills which are transferable and valuable in many different work and study

environments, thereby enabling students to explore their interests while keeping their options for progression open. As Diplomas have been developed with employers, universities and other stakeholders, the learning captures the relevance – and excitement – of the Diploma line.

(Department for Education UK 2013, p. 14)

However, as with Australia's 'earning or learning' policy, whilst such legislative measures may compel young people to remain in school, they do not address fundamental issues that lead to student disengagement and exclusion of students for reasons related to behaviour. There are clear links between schooling experiences and the sociocultural and economic circumstances in which young people grow up (Thomson 2002) that need greater attention from educational authorities. Restructuring the system of educational pathways is insufficient in itself to close the attainment gap between privileged and marginalized youth. In its final report on its pilot project around second-chance schools, the European Commission for Education and Training concluded:

> Failure at school affects all classes and groups in society, but not all of them equally. School dropout is not a socially 'neutral' phenomenon. It affects some groups more than others. Surveys show that dropouts often come from low-income families and there appears to be a strong inter-generational component in school failure. Many of these young people come from broken homes and only barely integrated immigrant and refugee families. Dropping out of school therefore is not an isolated phenomenon of learning failure. It is, like social exclusion, related to a multitude of social, health, family and financial factors. Although school failure is only one consideration in a larger 'domino effect' of social deprivation, dropping out of education is often the fatal stumbling block that deprives young people of skills, qualifications, purpose and order in life, as well as the social contacts and environment they need in order to be heard and appreciated. The fight against school failure is at the heart of the debate on educational reform. It is vital for a successful sustainable knowledge-based economy, a stable purposeful society and a democracy to which all can contribute.
>
> (2001, p. 4)

Thus, the success or failure of a society's most vulnerable youth affects us all. Drawing upon data from our research in Australia and England, we now introduce some of the young people whom we met in flexible learning centres. Their experiences help to provide insights into their reasons for leaving the mainstream and how and why they enrolled with alternative providers.

The flexible learning centres

The research sites for this project were purposively selected to represent diverse forms of alternative schooling within Australia and the UK. (See Appendix for more information.) The flexible learning centres in Australia included a church-funded high school for girls (Fernvale Education Centre) who were experiencing serious family and other personal problems; a regional flexible high school (Woodlands Flexi School) that was overseen by a local high school and supported by community organizations; a very small school (Cave Street Flexi School) located under a suburban house with one teacher and a social worker, catering to young people up to the age of 16, funded from small pockets of money from a variety of local high schools; an inner city school (Victoria Meadows Flexi School) enrolling young people from 15 to 25 years, co-funded by a church and a city council; and a learning centre (The Garage) that was primarily concerned with providing students aged 13–17 with work experience, mainly in relation to motor mechanics, funded by a large community organization. The two UK flexible learning sites were both registered schools. Ertonia Flexible Learning Centre operated across a number of different sites in a large English city, offering a number of GCSE courses along with various numeracy and literacy courses; those young people aged 14–16 had to be referred to the school by their mainstream school who subsequently funded their placements at the alternative site; others from immigrant or refugee backgrounds were often older. The West Canal Alternative School primarily catered to students aged 13–16 who were 'failing to thrive' in the mainstream and was located in a former town library; it was funded by local schools, a County Council and various social and community services; it offered students the opportunity to obtain vocational qualifications and to undertake some GCSE courses. The visits to each of these centres varied depending on the size of the site, but in most cases lasted up to a week in the first instance, often with follow-up visits, and involved observations and interviews (focus and individual) with young people, workers from the sites, and in some cases parents and former students.

Who attends flexible learning centres?

As we have indicated previously, much educational literature claims that factors such as social class, gender, race/ethnicity and sexuality are central to the vulnerability of certain young people (Connell 1993, 1994; Savelsberg and Martin-Giles 2008). Data from our study reinforce this. Fernvale Education Centre had a high Indigenous population and large numbers of young women who were mothers or expectant mothers. The gender balance of students at Woodlands was even and the students, who in the main came from rural backgrounds, were predominantly from low-income homes. Cave Street students tended to be young white working-class boys; there were five girls (out of twenty-one) in the school population. Students from Victoria Meadows came from a range of ethnic backgrounds, although white Australian students were in the majority, and many were living independently. The centre also catered to young mothers. The Garage student cohort was primarily male with a large Pacific Islander population. All the students at this centre came from low-income families. West Canal Alternative School was predominantly white working-class British, whilst Ertonia Flexible Learning

Centre had a very high Black working-class British population. Some students were returning to education after a long absence. Consequently, the age range of students sampled was quite broad – ranging from early teens through to early twenties.

Evidence from our investigations clearly supports the research that identifies broader socio-economic factors as being major contributors to young people's disengagement from mainstream schooling. For instance, we came across students who were, or who had been, highly transient, and/or homeless. For example, Terry from Woodlands Flexi School, stated that he 'moved out about two months ago . . . for about a month and then I moved back and I'm back with my mum now'; and a worker, Angela, from Victoria Meadows Flexi School made the following observation:

> We've got a couple of kids who have like very tentative housing arrangements – one kid that lost his house a few weeks ago was in a share house situation and then that fell apart then . . . he would have been homeless for a little bit and now he's kind of organized a meeting with someone's family. And another girl she was homeless for quite a while but now she's living with her boyfriend's mum and her boyfriend.

We also spoke to young people whose families were constantly on the move, making it very difficult for them to become attached to a school, as noted by Glen from The Garage: 'Well I've been to nine different schools, so yeah'. Julie, who attended Victoria Meadows, had experienced the same problem stating that she 'had been to eleven primary schools'. During one very unstable year she was required to move to three different schools. Much of our data support the contention that early school leavers have often experienced such family mobility, a factor that contributes to the social, emotional and academic disengagement from school.

Another factor that impacts negatively upon school completion is early parenthood. We met pregnant girls and girls who were young mothers who, despite government policies to the contrary, were, as in a UK study (Vincent and Thomson 2010), encouraged to leave school. Many of these young people, such as Julie, a student at Victoria Meadows, were also homeless or self-supporting. She explained:

> My mum left to go to Sydney when my daughter was four months old – and then my dad's never met my kids so . . . yeah I just, I moved into my boyfriend's house and his mum and dad supported me – and then yeah he's left.

In a similar way, the girls and young women who attended Fernvale Education Centre had experienced a wide range of difficult life circumstances that had left no room for schooling. Along with early pregnancies, some had experienced violence or sexual assault in the home and some were homeless. There was also a very high proportion of Indigenous students at the school whose experiences of mainstream schooling had been far from positive.

A number of young people found that due to family circumstances they had to begin work at an early age and this inevitably impacted upon their education. The following student found himself alone and trying to balance school attendance requirements as well as working to survive without family support:

> Malcolm (Victoria Meadows Flexi School): I left school about three months before I finished year 12. I got expelled because I had a pretty big personal conflict with my old school principal at Bielby Creek. Pretty much he told me that I was useless . . . I was working and he was like, 'you're not attending school' and I was working my arse off. I didn't have no parents supporting me because my parents are deceased and he didn't want to believe that they were deceased. I pretty much had to take in their death certificates to school to prove to him that they weren't alive . . . He would just pretty much, like I was just a dropkick of the community because I had no parents.

We also found one student, Patrick, a young man of 20, who attended The Garage, and was coping with fatherhood with the help of his family. He commented: 'Oh yeah, my son lives with me – me and the mother are still together but she works in Cairns' (approximately 1,800 km away). Those young people who were perceived as being 'different' by their peers provided accounts of the violence and harassment they had experienced at previous schools. Sometimes they were quite eloquent in their explanations of why this had happened. For instance, one boy from Victoria Meadows told us:

> Oh, just because I was different. I reckon people are scared of things they don't understand because, I don't know, they're just scared of it. They don't ask questions because they're idiots so they just resort to the one thing which gets them attention which is putting down on other people.

In contrast to such experiences, students often told us that there was little if any bullying in their current alternative schools (see also Evans *et al.* 2009). As a consequence of this along with a number of other factors, many students at these flexible learning centres often went to great lengths to attend lessons. Sienna from Fernvale, for example, who had two small children, noted: 'It takes me two and a half hours to get here'. Another young woman attending Woodlands surprised her parents with the same enthusiasm. Her mother, Joy, remarked:

> We live 30 kilometres the other side of town so I drive her. We leave home at six thirty . . . for her to put in that commitment, it's amazing . . . [her father] even said, he couldn't believe she's getting up at that time to get on a bus to get in here because he said, 'there's no way you'll ever get out of bed, you'll be late'. Now she gets up at five thirty and starts doing her hair!

These data suggest that whilst mainstream schools failed to retain these students, there are ways in which such young people can become (re)engaged, often enthusiastically, in schooling once their personal circumstances are factored into the educational context.

One of the great strengths of these flexible learning centres was that many of the structural reasons why young people might not be able to attend the centre were addressed by the school, and many of the students' previously unattended basic needs could be met by attending school. For instance, crèches and child-minding facilities were provided at some of the centres; bus fares for attending school were returned to students; all of the sites had food available for the young people; and there was support for dealing with the criminal justice system, for locating housing and for finding part-time work to support their return to education. Anecdotes such as the following, from Jane who attended Woodlands Flexi School, were not uncommon responses by students to questions about how the flexible learning centres might help them with outside issues:

> Yeah they definitely, definitely, definitely do that because there's this kid called Johnny and I think he like ran away or something and they like gave him money to go down to the Salvo's to get some clothes and he has a shower here and everything, and they've got food here. Then they've got, there's like counsellor people and sometimes there are some people that come in and they talk to you.

Meeting the material needs of these young people was critical for ensuring that they could stay at school. However, this alone does not completely explain many of the young people's ongoing commitment to their education. While the backgrounds of the students were diverse, common elements included resolute life ambitions and a strong work ethic. Many of the students thus put a great deal of effort into attending school. Some juggled work and/or caring responsibilities while others travelled significant distances to maintain their connection to learning. During an interview with one young student it emerged that her daily trip to the flexible learning centre took 90 minutes (when the buses were on time). On the way to school she passed several other mainstream schools, the closest of which was just a five-minute walk from her home. Clearly there were highly motivating factors making her put up with a long trip on unreliable public transport every day to get to her chosen school. Data from this project reveal that hers was not an isolated case. The young people interviewed for this project frequently commented upon their renewed enthusiasm for learning and their willingness to travel long distances to their alternative schools. Another common factor amongst the students was their identification of what they liked about their learning centre and the features that inspired them to enrol and maintain attendance. These included the learning programmes, the environment, teaching strategies and relationships. The following section reviews our data around each of these elements.

The learning programmes

Once enrolled, there were opportunities for young people across the sites to undertake studies that would lead them towards employment or further study. For instance, at Woodlands Flexi School, students could obtain the Queensland Certificate of Education, through undertaking regular Queensland curricula. There was also a focus on learning work skills; for example, Woodlands ran a 'work on trial' programme providing opportunities to obtain experiences in local workplaces and also combined academic subjects with a programme focused on obtaining vocational certificates in retail and construction. The opportunity to obtain vocational qualifications was common across a number of the sites. At The Garage, in addition to opportunities to undertake regular curricula – taken up by very few young people – there was a programme which enabled young people to work towards an automotive certificate. Similarly at Victoria Meadows Flexi School, in addition to standard curricula, students had the opportunity to obtain barista and Responsible Service of Alcohol certificates to support part-time employment opportunities. Fernvale Education Centre ran a standard curriculum. However, there was a strong Indigenous focus within this curriculum due to the large number of Indigenous girls attending the school. Because of its size, Cave Street Flexi School was only able to offer a limited programme. Its focus was on helping students to complete basic literacy and numeracy requirements that would facilitate student access to senior secondary education and trade certificates.

Learning programmes within the schools thus varied depending on their context and clientele. Whilst they all offered various levels of flexibility in terms of structures, some centres were officially classed as 'schools', others as 'centres' and 'work sites'. Accordingly, there was a diversity of offerings and students had to seek out the site that would give them the best chance of fulfilling their goals. Students frequently commented on the need for greater access to such facilities. Vanessa, who attended Victoria Meadows Flexi School, was adamant that 'if they created more of these small schools – like say in just main suburban areas – then I reckon it would have a huge popular demand and kids would be saved from going down the wrong track'.

Most students talked of wanting to finish school – to complete years 11 and 12, some wanting to pursue tertiary studies. One of the sites we visited had developed a relationship with a local university. Ali, who attended Woodlands Flexi School, had her sights set on a tertiary pathway, commenting: 'The good thing is that in year 12, if you've been through year 11 and 12 you can do the Tertiary Preparation Programme which will get you into uni'. Other sites focused more upon year 10 courses (for example, in woodworking, automotive engineering, literacy and numeracy), and vocational education (for example, certificate courses linked to trade traineeships or apprenticeships). Work experience was a common feature of many programmes and students appreciated the more hands-on approach. There were, as mentioned earlier, also opportunities to do short courses to help with employment; for example, barista training, first aid courses and photography. Programmes offered at these flexible learning centres also included courses and activities that contributed to the personal development of their students. Art and music, music production, animation, photography, field trips, community service and a great variety of life skills such as cooking, sport and personal fitness were offered in varying degrees across the research sites. Tara from Victoria Meadows was very enthusiastic about her flexi school's offerings:

> The music programme has been consistently amazing and wonderful. They've had the right teachers at the right times . . . I think the big difference is the fact that they've got their basic maths and English classes, but they have this huge variety of art subjects.

Apart from the academic offerings, across all of the sites there were commonalities in respect to the environments that facilitated the engagement of young people. For example, the students at West Canal Alternative School were involved in a wide range of activities that included the Duke of Edinburgh Award and group goals that built relationships and fostered self-confidence. Elaine, one of the teachers, described what the school offered:

> It is a national curriculum that we do. It is a national curriculum that we follow but we kind of don't sell it to the young people as a national curriculum . . . at the start of the year you will get a piece of paper and we put it all up. We go around, 'Everything that you want to do in the next year, put it on that piece of paper.' So they write. Like, last year's lot went out to do a helicopter ride . . . and they raised their own funds [in a café] and they got to do the helicopter ride. So every year we try and do that; something that they all want to do. Running the café was part of the work skills qualification. So it came to a qualification to do it, and then they got a reward; and then they got right into the programme. So they raised the money to do the helicopter ride and they all got certificates for that.

Data from the sites in both England and Australia show that the flexible learning centres recognized the diversity of student population in terms of their personal circumstances and reasons for seeking more flexible learning arrangements. The following approach, adopted by West Canal Alternative School, exemplifies this:

> Elaine: Everything is individually planned. Each pupil is given an individual learning plan, individual timetable. It is a programme to fit around them because sometimes you get a pupil go, 'Every Thursday morning, I like to go to town with my mum to do this and this.' 'So, right, we will put you in on the Thursday afternoon. So then we don't mess up your system.' Because we know if we put them in the morning, they just won't come. So we fit it around them.

Thus, we contend that meaningful forms of education were facilitated by the practices of the flexible centres in our study. Young people were able to build individual pathways that were quite extraordinary given their difficult lives. Sometimes teachers had to convince the young people that the work they were doing was not 'second best'. For instance, Shirley from Ertonia told us how she often had to tell students: 'Look, the same GCSE that they are doing there, you are doing here.' She would then go on to tell them:

> You get more help here. Once you have got it, put your head down, get your work out, and then go back to school and say, 'look, I have got it.' They said you can't do it. That's what they have said to you. Put your head down; and everything we help you with.

The outcomes for students seemed to support this. Shirley went on to note that 'The year 11s who have left, about 95 per cent have gone into college. They found college places.' Underpinning such achievements were the flexible and inclusive environments of these schools that facilitated an atmosphere of supportiveness, respect and positivity.

The environment

The environments at the various centres all tended to be far more relaxed than those found in traditional mainstream schools. Issues in respect to attendance, uniforms, assessment deadlines and behaviour were handled with greater flexibility and an ongoing staff–student dialogue. In terms of attendance and assessment deadlines, for example, Kevin, a student from Woodlands Flexi School stated:

> Cause you get flexible hours here and stuff, if you're working then you can pick the day you need to do subjects on . . . I only do two subjects here, I'm only doing English and maths at the moment, I'm hopefully going to be doing full-time now.

A core aspect of all of the centres, many of which had waiting lists, was that attendance was voluntary. The centres did not appear to want to be sites which young people were compelled to attend. Both students and staff talked about their centres as communities. For instance, a social worker, Angela, from Victoria Meadows Flexi School indicated:

> We work from a framework . . . informed by adult education models so that . . . anyone who comes here has to *want* to come here. We can't operate with young people who *have* to come, who are mandated to come and who don't want to; it's okay if they're mandated and they want to, but it has to be that personal drive to come. So that's how we operate we say, 'Well, aren't you here because you want to be here and didn't you say that you wanted to do this?'

Shirley, a teacher at Ertonia Flexible Learning Centre, also emphasized the need to allow young people to settle in to their schooling environment:

> When they come to the interview, they have a timetable. What they will do is, if a child hasn't been in school for some time, a couple of months or a year, we will say, 'Okay, start mornings. Just come in for the mornings.' Because [it's] a long day for them to sit all of a sudden . . . 'After a week we will see if you can manage the afternoons.' We will either phase them in or sometimes someone will say, 'Look, I only like maths and English and ICT [information and communication technology].' So we will say, 'Okay, do that.' Sometimes, if they come for three lessons, it's better than not coming. When you start forcing them, they will just drop out again.

For the teachers and workers at these schools, building a sense of community was fundamental to ensuring that the young people remained in the educational programmes offered at each site. It was often suggested that this community was something that was not readily available in mainstream schools. For instance George, a teacher from Victoria Meadows Flexi School, shared this view about community:

> I think the other strength that this place offers is a place where difference is accepted, where alternative viewpoints are accepted, alternative lifestyles are accepted in a safe and respectful environment where your ability to succeed in academic endeavours isn't the be all and end all of you as a person.

Similar views were articulated by Frank, the manager at The Garage:

> I think generally speaking it is a place where they can get a feeling of belonging, where they can get a feeling that it's a place . . . to go that doesn't have that strict classroom-type feel about it. That they do have certain freedoms . . . [but] I call it education by stealth. The education's not spoon fed or forced down their throat. A lot of the education in literacy and numeracy and so forth is delivered out on the floor. If they've got to prepare a job for instance, I mean they're learning literacy. If they're working out the cost of a repair to a vehicle they're learning sums – numeracy.

As indicated by Frank here, positive relationships with the young people helped to ensure that they engaged with the school's curriculum. Juliet, the teacher from Cave Street Flexi School, likewise emphasized the importance of relationships:

> Well my number one thing that I've learnt here in order to gain their co-operation because many of them . . . are a bit anti-'teacher' – is, relationships first, number one . . . So establishing relationships – they respond to that very well. Some of them – it takes a while because they've lost trust, not only in maybe some teachers they've had, but also adults in general – home stuff and whatever. So once they know they're safe, it's consistency of treatment, so no screaming, no shouting from myself, or from the youth workers.

Caring about the young people individually was also seen as a strength of Fernvale Education Centre. When asked what the school offered the girls, a teacher, Kathy, stated:

> It gives them a face . . . it's because of the positive regard policy that we have here, even when you walk in you know, 'Hello, how are you, it's great to see you here. I haven't seen you for a few days it's great that you're back.' [Administrators] stress that to us all the time and, you know, really it's common courtesy – a smile. You know – 'How are you?' and reconnecting with the girls if they've told you something about one of their hobbies – 'Oh how did you go on the weekend?'

To some extent respect for the students means forgetting or ignoring their past, seeing this 'educational journey' as some of the workers referred to it, as a new start. Common to all these centres was the opportunity provided to young people to make a fresh beginning. This is exemplified in the following comment by Shirley at Ertonia Flexible Learning Centre:

> We normally say to them, 'Here, it's a clean slate. Whatever's happened at school, unless it's a danger to a member of staff, no staff/pupil are told that information.' That way, then everyone is – you know, if you don't know anything, they get a fresh start. So we normally say, 'You will have a fresh start. So it's up to you then to make the most of it.'

Pauline, the principal at Woodlands Flexi School made similar statements. For example, she told us:

> Now we do get students with a rap sheet, you know ten pages long of behaviour issues . . . and I'll say, I interview every student and I'll say, 'Look yep, yeah this is the past, okay, yeah all right I really want to talk about your future and I don't want to see this here' and then we sort of put that to the side and – 'Right, what do you want, why do you want to be here?'

Accepting students for who they are was a key feature of the philosophy at Cave Street Flexi School:

> Juliet (teacher): They like the attention, individual attention. They have some plans for themselves for the future. They like each other. They have fun when they come here. They have the right to smoke – some of them are quite addicted and can't go because the classes are two hours in length. Now I think that's really quite challenging to them. I mean, we do get up occasionally and go for a walk just around the classroom or outside – I mean, it's just really a car park! We negotiate smoke breaks.

Similarly West Canal Alternative School in England has a 'no label' approach. Students get a clean slate and teachers work hard to make sure that the young people address whatever personal issues they arrive with. As Elaine noted: 'From what we do with young people and how many we work with, I have never seen a school do it the same. We never give up. As a school, they always give up at some point.'

Respect was also something that the students noted as being present both between staff and students and amongst students as well, as noted here by Molly from Victoria Meadows: 'Respect . . . it's one [of] our four Rs. It's not a place where you can relax and be cool and do drugs and not do your schoolwork because that's *not* what we're about.' Additionally, support systems were significant at all of these sites; as Megan from Fernvale commented: 'If you're wanting to get away from your family problems you just come to school, you know you can talk to one of the teachers or one of the youth workers and just nut it out.'

At Woodlands Flexi School, it was suggested that treating the sites, like the ones described here, as places to send young people as punishment for not appearing to fit in with mainstream schools would be counterproductive. Pauline the school principal stated:

> You don't want it to be something where kids feel embarrassed to go to . . . you must be dumb or naughty. You want it to be an alternative education where you can come, choose the programme that you need to do to get to your goal – that's the key . . . We're not a dumping ground. We're not here about punishment. We're about you making the choice.

The positive focus of schools was also important, both in terms of young people feeling 'celebrated' (not just accepted!), and being able to relax in a positive environment. Ali who attended Woodlands was forthright in her praise, saying, 'Oh yeah everyone's pretty laid back . . . and we all talk to each other, and the good thing is there's no actual real bullying here.' Thus, the environments of these flexible learning centres provided supportive contexts for the delivery of their curricula. However, according to both staff and students, it was the teaching and learning relationships fostered within these sites that were cited as key factors in their success.

The teaching relationships

The relationships that were part of the broader environment in the research sites were reflected in the teaching–learning relationships within the various curricula offered. These relationships were identified by young people and workers alike as being central to the students' ongoing engagement in the learning processes at the sites as evident in the following exchange:

> *What do you think people do here that helps you to learn that didn't happen at other schools?*
> Amy (Fernvale Education Centre): They'll come [teachers/workers] and talk to you and check up on how you're doing. Like if you don't

understand something they'll come and help you and it's just, they're more supportive.

The issue of teacher–student relationships and the teaching strategies that flowed from them was a dominant theme within the data. At West Canal Alternative School there was a code of unconditionality that allowed young people to transgress and learn from their mistakes, knowing that they would always be given a second chance:

> Elaine: And we don't exclude anybody. They're never excluded from the school. We kind of re-evaluate. 'Obviously this didn't work. What can we do to help you and make it better?' So we work closely with the pupils and the parents and agencies all the time. They get quite attached because they know that no matter what they do or what they say to you, that every morning they come in and you are still smiling; whatever they said to you yesterday, you are not going to carry it on to the next day.

The evidence derived from this study shows that for young people who are most at risk of dropping out, it is the emotional labour of the teachers and workers that often made a difference. Students frequently used adjectives such as 'caring', 'small', 'community', 'family', 'respectful', 'equal', 'supportive', 'non-judge-mental', 'mutual responsibility' when discussing their school. Katrina, a student at Fernvale Education Centre described her site as: 'Extremely different, extremely different (from previous school) because . . . you can go to anyone when you have a problem. It feels like a big family rather than just, you know? A thousand students all clumped together!' Across all flexible learning centres, workers and teachers allowed and encouraged students to call them by their first name. This practice definitely seemed to contribute to a breaking down of teacher–student barriers as shown here, as noted by Vanessa from Victoria Meadows:

> We get called by our first name and we call them by their first name so it's like an equal ground and it makes it so much more easier to connect and be more friendly with them than calling them Mrs or Mr.

The pedagogy that flowed from close teacher–student relationships seemed to engage and motivate students as exemplified by the following excerpt:

> *What are the main ways that this is different from mainstream schools?*
> Sam (Victoria Meadows Flexi School): It's just a lot more relaxed. I mean you've got your assessments and your assignments to do but it's not like if you don't do them you're gonna fail completely – no, you can come back and you can do it again. I mean you've got time to do things.

Many students commented on the effectiveness of teaching strategies that they described as 'real life', 'hands on', 'connected' and 'conversational'. Teachers gave them sufficient time and assistance to complete their work, as noted by Corey from Cave Street Flexi School:

> They're a lot more personal and they sit there and help you out and they have time to go round and check on different people and where they're at. And everyone's at a different level so it's not like you have to keep up with people. You go at your own pace so it's easier to work instead of like trying to keep up.

However, we do not suggest that these sites were without their tensions and conflicts. What was very different from mainstream models of behaviour management was that the teachers in the flexible learning centres were always very conscious of the personal contexts of their students; and they had devised flexible approaches for defusing emotionally charged situations; giving young people 'time out' and asking them to return to school the next day were common strategies:

> Pauline (Principal Woodlands Flexi School): So really we don't have a behaviour management problem – if kids misbehave here I'll always talk to them – 'What's going on today? Did something happen at home?' – And generally, 99 per cent of the time they've had a bad day, had a fight with mum before they came or something happened and we will just tell them, look go home. That's our behaviour management policy – 'Go (and) when you're ready to come back and learn, *come back*, and we have a re-entry interview' – so they come back to school and we just discuss it before they go back into class. So we don't really let situations blow up to the point where it becomes conflict. We just say, 'Look you're not ready today, go home.'

One of the young people in the project made the comment that there needs to be more schools like these. We broadly concur, but with a number of reservations. Our concluding thoughts sum up competing arguments in respect to this dilemma.

Conclusion

From our research there is a lot of positive evidence to support the argument that there should be more flexible learning centres. For many young people who had been marginalized from the mainstream schooling sector, the sites we visited provided a second chance to (re)engage with education in positive ways. Such opportunities are critical to re-engage young people in education and to advance their futures. It is especially important in Australia and the UK where the relationship between non-completion and unemployment is stronger than in many other OECD countries (AIG and DSF 2007; OECD

2011). Thus, as the Australian Industry Group (AIG) and Dusseldorp Skills Forum (DSF) (2007, p. 20) report *It's crunch time* indicates, providing opportunities for young people disengaged from the education system has to be 'a policy priority'. We and others (Thomson and Russell 2007, 2009) agree but would also argue that it is essential to foreground the *entitlement* of *all* young people to a high-quality education with broad choices for those who may be marginalized and disengaged. The flexible learning centres discussed in this chapter provide some indication of how such goals might be realized. As with other research (e.g. Alexander *et al.* 2001; White and Wyn 2008), our study indicates that the socio-economic factors that shape the life circumstances of young people do have a significant influence on schooling experiences and educational success. What made the sites studied here stand out was the way in which they recognized the difficult social and economic circumstances faced by many young people who were early school leavers. Hence, for example, they provided crèches and social workers and employed specific support workers, for example, Indigenous staff, to help their students find homes and to negotiate with welfare agencies. This recognition of the broader social factors that often contribute to early school leaving meant that many of the students were provided with the conditions that enabled them to attend school.

However, by itself such practical support, whilst extremely important, would not have been sufficient to keep these young people at school. Attention was also given to creating school structures, curricula and pedagogy that made the schools attractive to the students. Such conditions have been widely recognized as critical for re-engaging young people in education (AIG and DSF 2007). The structures within these schools acknowledged, for example, that there were often life circumstances that required flexibility of attendance; recognized that many students were addicted to nicotine and required time off the premises to smoke; and that having young people involved in decision-making, not having uniforms and being able to call the adults by their first names helped to create an environment where students felt like equal but different partners in the teacher–learner relationship. The curricula provided sought to support students obtaining part-time work, through short courses such as barista training, whilst also providing students with opportunities to obtain year 12 matriculation, university entry, vocational qualifications and life skills. This 'flexible pathways' approach was a key recommendation of a report commissioned by the New South Wales Department of Education and Training (NSW DET) published in 2005. In order to facilitate student engagement in meaningful learning, the report advocated the need to 'provide flexible pathways and enable students to exercise greater control over their own learning' (NSW DET 2005, p. 290). Moreover, the report argued for a more holistic approach to education via partnerships of government agencies, industry and community.

Such a full service philosophy of education was clearly evident at our research sites. Also fundamental to this philosophy was the supportive web of relationships amongst staff and students. Our data show that the pedagogical relationships within each site encouraged student reconnection to learning. Across the various sites, young people suggested that the relationship with workers and teachers was a key factor in their enthusiastic engagement with the curriculum. They also suggested that the quality of this relationship had been compromised in their mainstream schooling experiences. This is perhaps not surprising, as the AIG and DSF (2007, p. 23) report states: 'Our systems are relatively good at identifying curriculum standards but weak at constructing and supporting the personal and classroom relationships so crucial to productive learning.' For students in the middle years (when the possibility of disengagement is heightened) strong bonds with teachers have been shown to be particularly important (NSW DET 2005; Pendergast and Bahr 2010). Thus, whilst the teachers and other workers at the sites sought to make the curricula relevant or connected to the lifeworlds of the young people, they also worked on developing a positive emotional connection between themselves and the students; they opened up opportunities for students to engage with new knowledges and they valued the diversity of the student body of the school. The relationships developed through these practices can, as the AIG and DSF (2007, p. 35) report suggests, be 'life changing'.

However, despite the positive outcomes and practices of many of these flexible learning centres, we are concerned that creating more of them in the current neo-liberal climate might actually work against the provision of a socially just schooling system. While the data indicate that many students attending these sites would not be engaged in schooling if it were not for the existence of these alternatives, the creation of more such places may lead to a further differentiated system that works against severely marginalized students. Evidence indicates that they are often seen as 'dumping grounds' for struggling, disengaged and/or disruptive students (Kim 2011). Under the mantra of school choice, schools are constantly being differentiated with labels such as academies, excellence, vocational and the like. So-called 'free schools' in England and elsewhere purportedly offer to raise attainment whilst reducing inequality and providing parental and community schooling 'choices' (Hatcher 2011). However, they have the potential to fuel market competition with existing local schools, resulting in a loss of funding. In Sweden, many such schools are owned and operated by private companies seeking to make a profit (Sahlgren 2011). Some members of the British Conservative Party have looked to emulate the Swedish model:

> The country that provides the closest model for what we wish to do is Sweden. Over the past 15 years, Sweden has introduced a new system that has allowed the creation of many new high quality state schools that are independent from political control. All parents have the power to take their child out of a state school and apply to a new independent state school. The money that went to the failing state school is transferred to the new independent school. All the new independent schools are free. They are not allowed to be selective . . . These are the basic dynamics we will introduce into the British school system.
>
> (British Conservative Party 2008, p. 16)

However, the idea that a competitive, market-based system of school choice addresses educational disadvantage has been problematized by research. For example, Lubienski *et al.* argue that:

> [In] Detroit, profit-oriented charter schools, behaving like business enti-ties, are apparently willing to pay premiums to locate in more affluent neighborhoods. While initially focusing on areas with greater needs, even mission-oriented charter schools increasingly appear to target students in more advantaged neighborhoods where they can maximize market advantages but avoid 'undesirable' students. In these cases, both types of charter schools increasingly ring areas with higher concentrations of need. In this way, they are likely to serve more advantaged students who live near the schools while effectively limiting access to students from more distant, poorer neighborhoods – except, presumably, those students whose families have the means and desire to overcome such barriers.
>
> (2009, pp. 639–640)

Therefore, we argue that the ability to access real educational choices depends upon a range of social and cultural capital that may be lacking on the margins of society among populations affected by factors such as poverty and its attendant problems.

We also contend that the creation of non-mainstream, potential 'dumping grounds' of 'second chance'/flexible learning centres is not the answer to educational disadvantage. We certainly applaud the work being done for young people in these sites, but we also believe that their very existence allows main-stream schools to abrogate their responsibility towards their disengaged and most disadvantaged young people. The construction of more flexi schools, or second-chance schools as options for young people who are struggling in mainstream schools may well lead to a situation where students who do not fit the mould of a 'good' neo-liberal subject are forced to 'choose' this option. It is time to progress the case that it is the responsibility of *all* schools to provide a quality education to *all* of their students. The teaching practices and policies in our research sites provide a way forward if the mainstream is prepared to listen, and, most importantly, change how it goes about the business of educating young people in the twenty-first century.

In our research with these flexible learning centres we became aware of the way in which they were addressing the economic and recognitive injustices that many of the young people attending them had faced in their previous schooling and in their lives outside school. We address this in detail in Chapter 6 with case studies of Victoria Meadows and Fernvale. However, whilst young people were in the main very positive about their flexible learning centres, there were also some occasions when we felt that Fraser's (2010) concern with representative justice was not being addressed. Indeed we observed one instance at Woodlands Flexi School where one boy tried to affect a decision made by the principal because he claimed it was likely to make the centre more like a mainstream school.

His sense of frustration with having no avenue to challenge the principal, apart from a quiet chat in an office which we were allowed to observe, clearly affected his sense of belonging to the school. As a consequence, in our intent to explore the margins of mainstream education for lessons about how to create a government system of schooling that was underpinned by the principle of social justice, we also looked to schools that had a stated commitment to democratic governance. The majority of the schools we identified for this purpose were quite different from the flexi-learning centres considered in this chapter in that they charged fees and primarily catered to young people from middle-class backgrounds. However, they were clearly on the margins of conventional understandings of schooling and, we would suggest, due to their commitment to breaking down hierarchies between teachers and students, to encouraging participatory school governance practices and to rejecting arbitrary rule-making, they also have something to offer to a conversation about socially just schooling. We turn to these schools in the following chapter.

4 Democratic schools
Students and teachers working together

In the previous chapter we considered the reasons why some young people chose flexible learning centres to re-engage in learning. In this chapter we have a focus on a set of alternative fee-paying schools located in the UK and Australia. These schools offered an alternative to the mainstream primarily, although not exclusively, to young people from more middle-class and more settled backgrounds than the flexible schools. The three research schools that are drawn on for this chapter have a range of commonalities. They did not have a uniform, teachers were called by their first names, the young people had a great deal of freedom in determining how to express their views and identities and many of these students had chosen the school after having had a bad experience in their mainstream school. However, there were some significant differences amongst the schools in terms of size, philosophies and cost. Whilst we have reservations about young people leaving the government school sector for the private, we do think that schools such as these have some lessons to offer to the public sector.

In offering up these lessons we are mindful of the ways in which many government schools have been seeking to mirror the elite independent sector in response to a 'falling standards' discourse (Connell 2011). We reject such a view and are committed to a government sector that provides the best possible education to all young people. Indeed we do not think that there should be an independent school sector that is funded, even partly, by government. We are thus in agreement with Fielding and Moss (2011) who in arguing for the common school, not standardized schooling, but schooling that is open to all, express the view that the private schooling sector inhibits the provision of a socially just and democratic education. Further, we are of the view that many elite independent schools are authoritarian and provide their students with a distorted education (Connell 1993). Fielding and Moss suggest that such schools have no place in a democratic society. We agree. This does not mean that we are not sympathetic to many of the aims of independent schools such as those considered in this chapter. However, our major concerns rest with the health of government schools, and we are in agreement with Beane and Apple (1999, p. 5) who claim that 'public schools are essential to democracy'. However, apart from a few instances (for example, Mills 1996, 1997), we have seen little evidence of democratic schooling within most government schools and have been regularly confronted with practices in Australia that promote and indeed valorize 'undemocratic schooling' (Teese and Polesel 2003).

At the current moment then, in places such as the UK and Australia, we are a long way from a government schooling system that is underpinned by principles of social justice and democratic education. As we indicated in the Introduction, we are not intending to suggest here that many working in government schools are not seeking to provide a more democratic education, nor that some government schools have not been successful in providing more inclusive and respectful forms of education to their students (see Apple and Beane 1999a; Wrigley *et al.* 2011 for examples). However, government schools are rigorously policed by powerful neo-liberal discourses that valorize particular student constructions and governance structures, both of which do not sit comfortably with a democratic ethos. Indeed, as Beane and Apple (1999, p. 3) note 'the idea of democratic schools has fallen on hard times'. They point to the ways in which standardized curricula, academic outcomes, standardized assessment scores, privatization, teacher competence, the construction of students as human capital and discourses about falling standards in relation to student behaviour all contribute to a regulated and, indeed, fearful school environment; especially within schools in danger of being labelled as 'failing' or in need of 'special measures'. Such environments are often not conducive to democratic practices which have the potential to challenge the dominant neo-liberal framing of the purposes of schooling. Interestingly, the schools discussed in this book serve the needs of a large number of students who have been forced out of or have fled mainstream environments because of this very framing.

The schools considered in this chapter are often described, by themselves or others, as democratic because of their governance structures. A concern with what constitutes a democratic school has a history stemming from the early part of last century (see Dewey 1916; Beane and Apple 1999; Fielding and Moss 2011). One of the problems though, is that, as Woods and Woods (2009b) indicate, 'democracy' is a contested term with multiple meanings that shift and change in response to differing political climates (see also Perry 2009; Black 2011). At times democracy is framed within economic terms and associated with market freedoms and the right to choose. Our concern in this chapter is with democracy as a method of governance; a method that in terms of education has implications for school organization and classroom practices. However, what constitutes democratic governance is also not always clear.

For example, a distinction can be made, as Fielding (2013) does, between representative and participatory democratic practices. It is perhaps representative democracy that attracts the greatest focus in contemporary schools. In terms of curriculum, students learn, for instance, about voting procedures and organization in the Westminster system, the history of Western democratic government and about some of the threats to democracy. Most engagement in democratic practice is through organizations such as student representative councils, the membership of which, along with key decisions, requiring the approval of staff and/or the school administration team (Black 2011). Within this understanding of democratic education, there is an underpinning intent to prepare young people for participation in a representative democratic society. Such intent treats the student as a citizen in the making, rather than as a present citizen. It also works to construct this citizen as somebody whose major contribution to the working of society is through the ballot box in election years. In critiquing this production of the future democratic citizen Biesta has stated that it:

> entails an individualistic approach to democratic education, one in which educational efforts are focussed on equipping individuals with the proper set of democratic knowledge, skills and dispositions, without asking questions about individuals' relationships with others and about the social and political context in which they learn and act.
>
> (Biesta 2007, p. 742)

We suggest that a more participatory approach would involve asking such questions. We would also contend that the schools considered in this chapter, to varying degrees, present examples of such an approach in that they provided their students with opportunities to be an active participant in decision-making processes that affected their lives within the school and, via various overseas projects and international connections, afforded them the chance to exercise influence in the broader community. For example, Feldspar was an active member of the European Democratic Education Community (EUDEC) and St Ebenezer had developed relationships with charitable organizations in India (see discussion later in this chapter). We suggest that such connections and activities demonstrate to students the power of democracy-in-action for the good of the broader community.

Biesta (2007) also makes a distinction between education *for* democracy and education *through* democracy. Education for democracy is concerned with providing young people with the knowledge, skills and dispositions for future engagement in the democratic processes and as such aligns with concerns with representative democracy (see for example, MCEETYA 2008). Education through democracy, on the other hand, aligns with a participatory democratic philosophy in that it situates young people within the school in such a way as to learn to participate in democratic processes in the present. Education for democracy is largely tied up with curriculum and pedagogical issues. Education through democracy is largely related to the governance and decision-making structures present in schools.

This is not to say that the curriculum is not important for participatory democratic approaches. The curriculum is a key component of all forms of democratic education. Within many curriculum documents, for instance, there is an articulated concern with ensuring that students acquire an understanding of democracy and indeed even with what it means to be an active citizen (see for example, MCEETYA 2008). However, as many critical curriculum theorists have noted (for example Connell 1993; Apple 2004; Pinar 2004; Yates and Grumet 2011) what is designated as the official curriculum is a political decision which excludes certain perspectives. In most instances the official curriculum is one which presents knowledge as fixed and from the perspective of the dominant. Within such a framework the ideal citizen (with some notable exceptions, for example, Ghandi, Emily and Sylvia Pankhurst, Martin Luther King and Nelson Mandela) is usually constructed as one who aligns with the expectations of living in a representative democracy. However, we want to stress that whilst the focus of this chapter is on the decision-making structures in the schools and with the social relationships that make up these governance structures, we share the sentiments of Fielding and Moss (2011) who indicate that democratic schools are also concerned with rich understandings of what it means to be an active participant in the social and political worlds. Such understandings we recognize ought to also be the concern of both curriculum and pedagogy (Hayes *et al.* 2006).

One of our concerns with a focus on the curriculum and education for democracy is that, as indicated earlier, it is largely future orientated and concerned with young people as future citizens. Little concern is given to the present and the everyday of students. As Apple and Beane (1999b) indicate: 'the most powerful meaning of democracy is formed not in glossy political rhetoric, but in the details of everyday lives' (p. 120). Fielding and Moss (2011) also emphasize the importance of 'everyday democracy' when they provide a critical understanding of democracy as, 'a way of thinking, being and acting, of relating and living together' (p. 42). When the 'everyday' is taken into account the relationships within the student body and between teachers and students need to be considered. This we would argue is a feature of educating through democracy. Furthermore, we suggest that within this approach to democratic education, students are encouraged to look beyond the school to participate in addressing inequities and undemocratic practices and processes in broader environments. Biesta (2007) indicates that a democratic education entails a dual educational responsibility, 'a responsibility for each individual and a responsibility for the "world," the space of plurality and difference as the condition for democratic subjectivity' (p. 761). This approach, he indicates, draws up a 'political conception of democratic subjectivity'.

In foregrounding the schools here, we are recognizing the validity of a politics that seeks to challenge the legitimacy of existing institutions by building alternatives that model possibilities of what could be (Wright 2010). The independent schools in this chapter are alternative in the sense that they reject the governance structures of both the mainstream government and private sectors. Indeed, to some extent and to varying degrees, they could be regarded in Raymond Williams' (2005) terms as 'oppositional'. Whilst many of the young people attending these schools have, often in conjunction with their parent or carers, made a philosophical decision to attend an 'alternative school', many others are doing so as a result of a negative set of experiences in mainstream schools. Central to the organization of these schools is the philosophy that young people are capable of making key decisions about their environment and education, and that the making of mistakes is a learning experience in itself. Ironically though, in providing an account of the benefits of such schools we are in some sense hoping to undermine the need for their existence as we would like to see many of their practices becoming commonplace in all schools.

The schools considered here are located within a tradition of democratic schooling often epitomized by Summerhill in the UK (Neill 1970). For instance, in some of the schools, students voted on who was allowed to enrol at the school and on the employment of new teachers; some schools held meetings where individual teachers and students had equal voting rights and the same freedoms to speak; and in some schools students were trusted to determine classroom attendance according to their needs. The benefits of this student-centred approach to schooling included young people's sense of ownership of the school, of responsibility for themselves and others, of self-confidence and worth, and a commitment to the principles of active citizenship. However, this approach was not without issue. For example, it could take some students a long time to assume personal responsibility for engaging in learning; some school meetings had the potential to damage individual students who became the focus of the meeting; the making of rather trivial decisions took up significant periods of the school day; the effect on teachers could be frustrating as some students did not turn up for classes; teachers were made to accept decisions which had implications for their classroom practice; and time appeared to be being wasted.

This chapter is framed up similarly to Chapter 3 in that we consider who attends these schools and their reasons for doing so. However, we then explore the different ways in which each of these schools addressed governance issues. The three schools, whilst having some strong commonalities, also have some major differences in terms of governance. St Ebenezer, whilst consultative with the students, had a Board of Governors and was heavily influenced by its history shaped by a Quaker ethos; Distincta College worked with a philosophy of no rules and consulted students on key decisions, but final power rested with the school principal; and Feldspar, which we consider in more depth in Chapter 6, drew on the principles of direct democracy with all students and teachers having an equal vote on all decisions.

The students: who attends and why?

The students who attend these schools are diverse. However, due to the fees charged, the schools tended to be selective in their enrolments. Thus, one of the critiques of such schools is that they primarily cater to middle-class students who can afford the fees (Ashley 2009). This appeared to be the case with two of these schools, Feldspar and St Ebenezer. Indeed, at Feldspar teachers indicated that they would struggle to be able to pay for their own children to attend. The same would have been true at St Ebenezer except for a special provision entitling teachers to reduced fees for their children. Indeed, one teacher at St Ebenezer told us that his sister, a former pupil, who was now a veterinarian could not afford to send her children to the school despite veterinarians being, as he said, 'fairly well paid'. However, Distincta College appeared to be quite flexible around fees in order to ensure that a wide range of students could be enrolled. For example, a number of students told us of how their parents had negotiated the school fees down in order for them to attend the school. These stories were reinforced by the staff.

Of the three schools, only St Ebenezer gave the impression of being a wealthy school. It had large playing fields, excellent facilities and classrooms, an extremely pleasant dining area and an impressive entrance foyer. However, the deputy headteacher, Lyn, wanted us to know that the school was very different from other independent schools in the UK. This, she said, was apparent in the student population who were not 'stereotypical of a type of the middle-class child' in that, 'they've got their eyes open'. The other two schools did not appear to be as wealthy as St Ebenezer. Students at both Distincta College and Feldspar complained about aspects of their school's physical features and structures. However, students at both Feldspar and Distincta indicated that their attendance at the school was not about purchasing a particular physical environment, but about experiencing an environment in which a particular philosophy of education was being articulated. The ability to purchase such a philosophical environment did however have an impact upon the composition of the student population. This was often recognized by the schools. For instance teachers and students alike at Feldspar commented upon the unique nature of the local population from which students were drawn. The part of England in which this school was located was widely recognized as supporting middle-class alternative lifestyles. As one teacher told us, 'The other important thing to remember about Feldspar is we're in a very middle class, very alternative bubble.'

That parents had a commitment to alternative education was a theme running through many of these schools. For instance, at Distincta, 15-year-old Mia told us how there was a history of alternative education in her family. She noted that her father had gone to an alternative school in Scotland, 'with the whole sort of no rules, self-motivated learning', and as a consequence was 'keen on something like that for us as well'. Many of the students we interviewed at St Ebenezer were the children of parents who had attended the school and who had wanted their own children to experience the freedom of this school. Many of the teachers we spoke to were also committed to the ethos of the school and sent their own children to the school.

The students at each of these schools were not necessarily high achievers. There were students at all three schools who told us about their own struggles with learning. At St Ebenezer numerous teachers and students told us about the large numbers of students with dyslexia that they were now attracting. Many of the teachers indicated that they were proud of the reputation they had for addressing the needs of diverse students. One teacher stated that what she liked about the school was that, 'it's normal to be different'. When we were talking about the school's reputation with some year 12 girls, they told us how a previous headteacher had tried to limit the number of special needs students coming to the school, but had faced serious opposition from parents and students alike.

They suggested that this had been the reason for his eventual departure from the school. One girl, who was defensive of the school's reputation, complained about the way that the number of students who came to the school with 'special needs' was used to denigrate the school. Sarah from year 12 stated that along with being seen as a 'hippy school':

> We're just seen as lots of rich kids who can't work because the school we come to, because the school's known as sort of a special needs school. And it's not a special needs school entirely and we're not all rich kids and it's a bit annoying.

The aspirations of the students across the schools were varied. Whilst many did aspire to be engineers, doctors, lawyers, film-makers and to enter other professional and creative industries, many also expressed desires to be chefs, make-up artists and to take up various trades. It was only at St Ebenezer where we experienced an assumption that students would go on to university, with students in the upper grades often naming Oxford and Cambridge as their destinations of choice. However, whilst many of the students we spoke to appeared to have very comfortable lives, this was not the case across the board. Affluence can bring about its own set of problems. One teacher told us about how some students, especially the boarders, felt like they were being 'dumped' at the school. For instance, we were told about one girl with serious emotional issues whose father's personal assistant made all of the arrangements for her holidays and days out.

In all of the schools there was discussion about the types of students that the school suited. Whilst it was widely recognized in all three of the schools that they provided an alternative for those young people who had not coped well in the mainstream, there were some concerns expressed about the ways in which some students might not settle well into their new school. This concern was articulated by both students and teachers. For instance, teachers and students both indicated that at Feldspar those students who seemed to settle well into the school were those who came in the first year of high school when they were 11. One teacher from Feldspar, Ava, argued that in many cases when they came at 14 or 15 they were in a mindset where they saw teachers as authority figures or tried to test the limits of the freedom available at the school. She stated that:

> The freedom can be very daunting. Some children come and they can do nothing for a month and that's quite tricky for us because that's what we're all about, we're about choice, we're about taking responsibility for that choice but we also don't like children doing nothing because it's deeply, it's just not good, they get up to mischief, it's not educating them, they're, yeah, it's not good doing nothing.

Some of the students at St Ebenezer also talked about the need for students to be self-disciplined and not to exploit the freedoms that they had at the school.

However, as one student, Scott, told us: 'Usually they do reach a point where they, they kind of tone it down.'

Whilst many of the students attending these schools had made the school their first choice, usually in consultations with their families; many had also turned to these schools as a consequence of some form of dissatisfaction with a previous school. These dissatisfactions included bullying, feeling oppressed by rules and regulations, and being alienated by the curriculum and pedagogical practices. Their new schools were seen as providing a remedy to these concerns. In considering why students had chosen their alternative school, as in the previous chapter, we also raise some of the critiques that students had of the mainstream sector.

Many of the students who attended these schools had come from both private and government schools. Evan, a year 11 student at Distincta, who had been at the school since year 7, had been given the option of a Catholic boys' school but had chosen Distincta because when he visited the school for a trial day he had decided 'it was a nicer environment and atmosphere'. Some of the students at St Ebenezer even talked about how they had been considering Eton, but their parents had been much more supportive of this school's relaxed environment. There were students at all three schools who had previously attended Steiner schools but had found them wanting in some regard (see Ashley 2009 for a discussion of Steiner). For instance, 14-year-old Paige at Feldspar told us how she had been at a Steiner school for seven years. She went on to say:

> I found it okay when I was younger but when I started to get older I felt quite restricted and, yeah there was quite a lot of rules and, I was generally not that happy and difficult things happening with friends and things like that.

Ruby, a 17-year-old who had been at Distincta since the end of year 7, had tried a secondary college following primary school. This she said had not been a good experience: 'I didn't like the mainstream schooling system and I like to have a certain amount of freedom.' Mia in year 10 had come to Distincta in year 8 from a government school because the 'factory-like system of school' did not suit her.

Many of the reasons given by the Feldspar students for coming to the school also related to a particular critique of mainstream schooling. For instance, some of the students at Feldspar had formerly been to private schools where they had found the expectations and rules more restrictive than was comfortable for them. For instance, 14-year-old Holly, from Feldspar, had tried various forms of schooling prior to attending the school, including home schooling. Her previous school had been a private one where 'they expected a lot of you and I couldn't handle the work'. As a consequence of her unhappiness at the school she told us that: 'Mum decided it would be better for me to go here because it's a lot less stressful.'

At St Ebenezer, Eric in year 7 decided to move to the school because he had been 'bullied quite badly' at his previous schools and that at St Ebenezer bullying was 'pretty much non-existent'. He told us that he had been to three different schools and this was 'the best one I've been to, definitely'. As with the flexible learning centres, bullying at a previous school was a theme that cropped up over and over again as a reason for leaving the mainstream. Dennis, a 14-year-old, told us he had come to Distincta for this reason. He then went on to tell us that Distincta often attracted those students 'who don't really fit in anywhere else, people who've decided they don't like how their school works and they want a different experience'. Whilst students regularly claimed that bullying did not occur at their current schools, this did not mean that there were never any conflicts between students. There were. However, it was the ways in which such tensions were addressed as a whole school that was significant. We cover some of these processes below in the section on governance. However, it is worth noting here that behaviour management at Distincta and Feldspar was largely dealt with through the school council and meetings. Ian, one of the teachers, when speaking about his induction into the culture of Feldspar, gave a sense of how behaviour deemed inappropriate was addressed better through the meeting processes within the school compared with his previous school:

> And I was so, so impressed with that and much, much better because it's their world and it's their issues and they understand them and they deal with them much better than any group of adults could've, 'cause we would've made a judgement about it from our perspective.

It was not just the relationships between students that appeared to be based on mutual respect, but also between teachers and students. This was apparent on various visits to the schools, both in the ways in which teachers and students spoke to each other and in their conduct. For instance, on one of our visits to St Ebenezer we were invited to stay for lunch by Robert the headteacher. We joined a table with a lone year 8 at it, who Robert introduced us to and who greeted Robert by his first name. We were later joined by other students who chatted freely with us about the school. Over and over again we were told how the teachers or workers at these schools treated the students as either friends or as equals. This contrasted with many of the students' previous experiences. Common amongst many of those students who had attended a previous high school was a sense of having had an adversarial relationship with teachers at that school. Sixteen-year-old Chris from Distincta had left his government school in year 8 because of always getting into fights with teachers because 'they were just really, I think, stuck-up and arrogant'. Twelve-year-old Bella had been to an exclusive girls' grammar school prior to coming to Distincta. However, she had left that school because she felt that she had been bullied by one of the teachers: 'Because I'm quite forgetful she told me that because I didn't bring my stuff sometimes I shouldn't bother to come to school.' Julian, a 16-year-old also from Distincta gave us an example of the kinds of events that had caused him to leave his secondary college, including spending a lot of time sitting outside the classroom for behavioural issues. He told us, 'since I've come here it doesn't take effort to go to school'.

As with the students in the flexi schools, respect was a key theme in the interviews with the students at Distincta. They referred to the respect they felt towards each other and to the teachers, and the teachers towards them. Similarly, calling teachers by their first names made a big difference to students. For instance, year 11 Kaylea at St Ebenezer told us:

> I think it's more like a community and like everyone knows each other there's no like, there's not even any difference between, like, the teacher status and the student status; it's more like *together* – like the way you can call them by their first names.

Whilst the positive relationships between teachers and students were mentioned regularly, there were some conflicts. In one focus group discussion with three students, Chris at Distincta told us:

> I don't get along with every teacher that well, as these two probably know (laughs) but I, you know, I can sort of talk to them about my problems I'm having with them and like sort it in the best possible way I guess . . .

What is significant here is that the difference of opinion was aired and that the student and the teacher both had opportunities to put their position to the other in order to reach a resolution.

Freedom was mentioned regularly by students at the three schools as a reason for being happy at their current school. For instance, freedom of expression through the non-uniform nature of the schools was something students at all of the schools valued. For example, one girl attending Distincta College, Alicia, had moved to Australia from a military base in Germany and she and her parents had wanted to find a school without a uniform and, apart from one selective high school, Distincta had been the only school that they could find. Madison, a year 7 student at St Ebenezer, also highlighted the non-uniform policy of the school as one of the reasons why she liked the school:

> I love the fact that we can wear whatever we want (laughs). We can really, like, express ourselves and stuff – like buy our clothes and you feel more comforted when you're wearing clothes from home. And I really like how we can talk to our teachers and call them by their first names. I think that's really nice – and it's a vegetarian school and I really like that too (laughs).

At Feldspar and Distincta students had the freedom to make decisions about their own learning which also involved deciding upon attendance at class. However, in both of these schools whilst there was no punishment for skipping classes there was an expectation that students would attend. For instance, Riley from Feldspar, when discussing the ways in which new students settled into the school, told us:

> I think some kids do have trouble kind of adjusting to being able to choose whether they go to lessons – even though actually when you sign up for a lesson you are meant to go for the rest of the term, that is, you have made a decision but, I mean, if you don't go teachers won't kind of chase you up and tell you, but it's not a rule that you're allowed to . . . It's just people don't want to have to cause that kind of trouble with forcing someone to come.

Alicia from Distincta noted that whilst attendance at class was not mandatory:

> It's pretty much like every other school that if you don't go to class you will get marked as absent and it'll look bad on your report. But if you, but if, but it's not like they're gonna, like, yell at you or you're going to get detention like at most schools, so it's a little more relaxed.

Other students, when asked how teachers at Distincta reacted if they did not turn up to class or school, indicated that they were often asked where they had been and why they had not turned up, but that this was always done in a supportive and non-blaming way. One student joked that when he was late for class 'my music teacher texts me asking where I am and demanding a latte with two sugars'. When asked if they might skip a lesson in order to work on an assignment for another subject, Julian from Distincta told us that this was possible, but not likely to happen because:

> It's just kind of, like, also not going to certain teachers' classes is disrespectful to them as well. And as we have a kind of friendship to the teachers if we ditch their class and not listen to them it's just disrespectful in a way.

At each of the schools, students provided examples of how they had been inspired by teachers or had been encouraged to think for themselves. Students at Distincta regularly commented on the ways in which Don, the school principal, had increased their enjoyment of mathematics. However, they also told us about the ways in which he stretched their thinking. For instance, during a focus group discussion students provided the following anecdotes:

> Julian: Well some classes Don doesn't even teach us maths, he teaches us life lessons and tells us stories and like, makes us think of the moral of the story and just – but he gives you, yeah he gives good life lessons; tells us, like, every single day 'getting a part-time job now is more important than school, you

need it because it gives you more experience than you'll ever get from school' (slight laugh) and stuff like that.

Ella: In our Latin class yesterday instead of making us sit down and do Latin he just wrote this saying up on the board, it's: 'work conquers all' and then spent the lesson talking about that.

Ryan: Sometimes we have arguments with him, you know friendly arguments. He'll come up with some sort of concept such as 'the earth is flat' or 'there is no air' and he'll argue that point against us. He's very good at it (laughs).

Julian: He teaches us to argue back. Actually Don's most common, like concept is, he wants us to think for ourselves. And he teaches us some sort of maths that get our minds to do that as well, and like, that's just the thing that he wants everyone to be able to think for themselves no matter what happens – it's being your own person.

Ian, a teacher at Feldspar, recounted to us how in relation to those subjects that were not part of the compulsory curriculum, the school philosophy had made him more 'creative'. He was now bringing some of these democratic methods across to the work that was part of the curriculum for GCSEs. Ian explained that he had wanted to employ the school's philosophy of democratic decision-making to both the content of the curriculum and to the assessment of student work. For instance, he told us: 'I make them make all the decisions about what their work is going to be on . . . they pick a theme for their project then they have to decide what a piece of work is.' What Ian found, as is indicated by much of the literature on high-quality pedagogies (see for example, Hayes *et al.* 2006; Darling-Hammond 2010), is that when more is demanded of students the more they rise to the challenge. He stated for instance: 'I was really impressed by the way a lot of the younger groups have really . . . come up with some incredibly creative work.' The students were then encouraged to assess their own work using a set of criteria developed by the teacher. This, he argued, provided them with a substantial understanding of what constituted quality work. In relation to his English teaching for GCSE, Ian pointed out that the students would have to do an analytical essay on a modern novel. He suggested that in many schools this novel would be set by the teacher or head of department. However, Ian tried a different approach:

I wanted to put that process over to the kids so what I'll do I'll go, I'll spend half a term on the process of choosing the novel they as a group want to study. So I'm not, I won't teach individual kids, individual choices for themselves; they have a responsibility within their community. So we'll start with twenty books and then they'll whittle it down to a long list of fifteen so then we'll study those fifteen in a bit more detail and then they'll get it down to five and then eventually democratically as a group they'll decide which book.

He then went on to say that even though he was the teacher and had a voice in the process, it did not unduly affect their decisions:

> There's some input from me because there are books, but I often don't get my way (laughs) – in fact, since, I've been doing that for about three or four years now and I've wanted to teach *Nineteen Eighty-Four*. And no bloody group has picked it yet (laughs).

For many of the students at these schools there was a sense that 'you have to be a certain type of person to teach here' (see Chapter 5 for further discussion on teachers in alternative settings). Whilst the students often argued that teachers did not need to teach differently, they did need to approach the students differently from in the mainstream as they did not have the same type of institutional authority. As such students indicated, for example at Feldspar, that 'I really have a lot of respect for all our teachers', with others chiming in, 'me too!' This was important for the students, as Evan from Distincta indicated: 'I find that the better the relationship I guess I have with the teacher the better I work.' However, there were times as in all schools when some students did not click with some teachers, as noted here by Mia from Distincta:

> You do get teachers who don't quite fit, so, like, Kelly was willing to listen but sometimes you get those who maybe just don't understand or they really struggle with trying to help, so I've ended up dropping a subject because I've just found it too infuriating (slight laugh).

Brian from the same school explained how teachers who did not fit in often did not stay at the school long. He told us about a German teacher who was not a 'Distincta' type teacher as she would just tell them to 'open the book, do this question' and spoke to students in disrespectful ways. He gave us an example:

> Some person left his bag in the classroom and during the class he just wanted to kind of sneak in and get it; she shouted at him, you know – and this school that's not – if somebody makes a mistake you don't shout at someone.

For many of the students attending Distincta, the school had brought about a dramatic change in the way they engaged with school. We often asked students at the end of the interview if there was anything that they would like to add. In one such instance, Nicholas wanted to make sure we realized what an impact the school had had on him. He told us:

> I just want to say I used to be horrible at everything I did, I never really did any work in primary school, I always used to just sort of sit and stare out the window whenever anyone asked me to do anything, and sort of Distincta's sort of changed all that. I actually enjoy doing the work now . . . and, like,

drama, I used to hate drama and not because of the teachers or anything I just did not enjoy it and now, I really enjoy it now.

Mia also wanted it made clear how much she felt she had benefited from the school:

> Another thing is my confidence. I don't know whether it's just growing up and maturing or whatever but, like, at my old school I was just extremely shy and really, really nervous about social interactions and stuff like that. And I come here and I've just noticed like over the last year or so I just feel a lot more confident sort of talking to people (laughs) and sort of doing presentations and stuff like that.

The students who attended these three schools, whilst primarily coming from a middle-class background, had not necessarily had an easy time with their previous schooling. Some had learning difficulties, some had been disengaged from learning, some had been bullied and some had had conflict with the authority structures of their previous school. Some, of course, had made their current school their school of first choice. Life was not always smooth at these schools; sometimes young people had conflict with teachers and sometimes each other, and sometimes they took a while to settle into the school, and indeed for some they would discover that the school was not for them. However, we were constantly told by the young people who had transferred into the school from another, more mainstream school that the transition had been highly successful. They felt more confident, more respected, more engaged and more enthusiastic about learning. For many of the young people who had only ever attended their current school they could not imagine wanting to be in any other environment.

The schools: experiments in democratic governance

The thread that binds these three very different schools together is their attempt to work with a governance structure that supports the input of students into key decisions. As with most democratic schools, it is in school meetings that major decisions are made. Meetings were used at the schools in various ways to address such topics as environmental concerns, organizational matters, behavioural issues, the enrolment of students, the employment of teachers, and even in one school, the salary of teachers. The system at St Ebenezer was highly structured reflecting a representative democratic form of organization, partly due to size, whilst at Distincta and Feldspar there was more of a direct democratic form of organization. We explore the role of the significance of school meetings at Feldspar here and in the chapters that follow.

St Ebenezer had a Quaker background, although it was never a formal Quaker school. We were told: 'The school was actually started by the theosophists who are a kind of Anglo-Indian religion so that's where the vegetarianism comes from.' The school was then bought by one current teacher's Quaker grandparents in the 1920s. The heritage of this was present in the governance of the school. We were told by this teacher, Steven:

> That's partly why we have the silence and the morning talks and things like that. But I mean, for instance, council meetings are Quaker – I don't know how much you know about Quakers . . . you sit around and wait for a consensus (slight laugh). You don't have formal votes. At our staff meetings we almost never have formal votes, I mean Colin [a former headteacher] or Robert [current headteacher] would kind of try and assess the feeling of the meeting on this and that.

The council system at the school consisted of elected representatives from classes, referred to in Quaker terminology as 'companies'. This council met two to three times a term and the only staff members who were allowed to observe were the headteacher, the deputy head and the bursar. However, these staff members were only meant to observe and to clarify any information that the council required in relation to any matter that they were discussing. This body then made recommendations that would then be taken to a whole school meeting which would either reject or ratify the proposal. Jake from year 7 explained the process to us:

> Yeah, so like, from every group, one person or two people are chosen so they can discuss with their group what needs to be changed and then they discuss it with the council and then after it's been passed they take it before the whole school at morning talk to see if everyone wants it.

Robert, the headteacher, gave one example of where some students had tried to make a change to the organization of the school day at council but had had this recommendation thrown out by the whole school meeting:

> They wanted to change the pattern of the school day so we have moving time between each lesson so there's a ten-minute break to give people a chance to sort of (laughs) get their books, go to the loo and move from one room to another; they wanted to shorten all of that, they wanted to shorten the day just by fifteen minutes because it would give the people who go to London time to get the earlier train blah-blah-blah. And it was quite well thought out and there was a big discussion about it; it got through council but it got thrown out by the school because they said, 'Look, this is a school for all of us and actually we quite like it as it is, we changed it only two years ago so, no.'

Robert explained that certain areas at St Ebenezer were beyond the jurisdiction of the students. These areas included financial and curriculum matters, although there were often financial implications associated with student decisions. As a number of students told us the council could make applications for funding. Lachlan in year 7, who had once been a councillor, told us about some decision-making that had occurred in the junior school in the previous year:

> Near the end, the school council were brilliant. They got us brand new water fountains and they argued for making a huge brand new climbing frame and everything so we got that done as well. And I think at the end of this year I think the tennis court down in the junior school is going to be resurfaced.

However, whilst the school meeting had the power to reject or ratify proposals from council, the headteacher did have the right to veto those decisions that were considered to be beyond the remit of students. Robert explained to us that this veto was only ever used as a last resort: 'I do have a power of veto over everything and I think it's been used, I think the veto's been used five times in the last twenty years.' He went on to explain that he had lunch with the senior councillors each week to discuss things with them in order to avoid being put in a position where he might have to veto a school decision. He told us:

> They shouldn't really put anything before the school that I'm going to have to veto. They should, through prolonged discussion work out a compromise or a way that they think is going to work for everyone.

The other two schools had quite different approaches. Feldspar, for instance, was quite explicit that no teacher had the right of veto in relation to any decisions made at the school meeting. The decision-making was slightly different at Distincta with the principal having a greater say over serious matters. However, both of these schools dealt with a range of complex matters that in most schools are the responsibility of teachers. Sometimes these meetings could be routine and be completed in short periods of time. However, when an important matter had to be discussed the meeting would be extended to facilitate a thorough engagement with the topic. Distincta did not have 'rules' that could be referred to when students were deemed to have done something wrong. The founding principal of the school, Don, explained to us why he did not want the school to have rules:

> People are always hanging out, 'give us a firm rule, give us something we can grasp onto and be clear about' and then they take anything you say almost and turn it into a rigidity which then becomes a problem. So it's almost like any philosophical statement, any rigid thing is going to be taken to an extreme and then there's going to be people who object to it strongly and then suddenly you've got two warring parties; the dominant one and the small disaffected one. So, I don't know how you get around that but I do know that I haven't been able at any stage to come up with stuff that's an absolute.

As a consequence, it was at the school meeting where students and teachers discussed the extent to which an event that had occurred warranted attention. During a focus group discussion involving Julian and Ryan, we asked how they would explain this philosophy of the school to prospective students. They responded as follows:

Julian: I would say that it's not a school for bludging; some people here they just go 'Oh we can come here and we can do whatever we want, you know it's no rules.' *No*. Like you need – I think the school is based around mostly respect and like, just mutual respect, and that's how everything gets along, and *trust*. And that's, I think that's just how the school co-operates and it has for a while.

Ryan: It can be hard to explain to people that we don't really have formal rules, but still explain that we have the responsibility of keeping the school going and putting in our part.

Another girl from Distincta also explained that not having rules did not mean that there was chaos at the school because there were 'expectations'. Mia told us:

I think we probably have more expectations than other schools, so in a sense we have more rules. But it's like, sort of trial and error expectations, so it's sort of like, you do it. If something goes wrong we discuss that rather than cutting it off and saying 'stupid you, you made a mistake I'm going to make you write some lines' . . . It's sort of a bit more sort of natural, sort of like, if you do something wrong, break our expectations, there are natural consequences for that which you have to deal with.

One student, Evan, described how one such instance of 'expectations' not being met at the school was addressed:

Like, we've had issues with students which affected the whole school, such as drinking on an excursion and we went through about nine hours of meetings within the course of . . . about, two or three – a lot of meeting hours in the course of about two or three days just discussing what the school could do, what the students could do and you got a whole range of different opinions from 'they should stay' to 'the students should be just kicked out immediately they're bad for the school'.

The vast majority of the students we interviewed highly valued the chance to provide input into key decisions at the school. Thirteen-year-old Alicia at Distincta noted how for significant meetings she had stayed at the school until after 6 p.m. She stated that: 'I think they're very important and they really work problems out.' When asked if she felt that students were listened to and that their views were considered seriously, she replied, 'definitely!' When asked to give an example, she used the case of making decisions about new students after their trial days:

> Mainly what big decisions we make is [about] trial day students, where we all get to talk about what they've done that day. And we get to vote on who gets to stay in and why, why not. And it's not like we can just randomly say 'we don't like that person' (slight laugh); we have to give a good reason. So I think that's probably one of the most important decisions of who stays and who doesn't.

Here, Alicia is referring to a process at the school whereby in order for potential students to decide whether they thought the school was for them and for existing students to consider if they should be accepted or not, potential students had to have a trial day, and sometimes even a trial week. Evan explained the rationale for this:

> The basis of that is that the class members will be spending the majority of the time with that student and so there's a say in that; whether they're going to be productive or destructive to the classroom and [the] community.

Then Ruby explained what students looked for with these potential students:

> I find, like, a certain amount of confidence is good, and if they seem kind of, if they're not violent and if they don't show just traits that immediately might make you think that they possibly could be more damaging to the school.

The meeting also appeared not to be a place where frivolous claims were brought up. We were told by one group of students that if they were having problems with other students they would 'use the meeting as a last resort'. Chris told us for instance that 'if someone's doing something I'll just pull them up by myself and have a word with them'. Nicholas, a 16-year-old whose only high school had been Distincta, agreed with him: 'I've never really had any problems with anyone in the school yet, but I mean if I did have any problems I would, the meeting would be the last resort, yeah.'

For those students who are 'brought up' at meetings it can be a difficult time, although many recognized this as not necessarily a damaging event. Evan from Distincta had been the subject of one of these meetings. He suggested that 'they can be hostile environments when people get really passionate about a topic'. He had been part of a group that had been drinking on camp. He described the experience as 'character building' and suggested that it was much more effective than being given a detention or being suspended from school. He described the experience:

> You're given a chance to respond to every single comment there is, which is important . . . I guess it's usually difficult because you have such a close

connection with each of those students, but if anything it's, I find it more of a positive influence than perhaps a detention or a suspension. Like with a detention, 'Okay I've been put in a room that hasn't really taught me anything'... If I'm being told by *all* of my friends and people I know or about 50 or 60 that what I've done is wrong, then I'm gonna take note of that and change my behaviours to suit that.

Another group of students told us about a series of events that had led to one student being asked to leave the school just prior to one of our visits. The students described him as 'an *incredibly* nice guy' who 'had a condition in his head' which meant that 'every now and again he'd have spurts of anger, like really big spurts of anger.' This boy was said to have brought a knife to school and had said that he wanted to stab someone and he had also been throwing things off a bridge and on to a highway. As a consequence a whole school meeting was called to address this behaviour. Whilst the students generally liked the boy, they did not know if they could trust him, noting 'we kind of reached that decision at the end of the meeting'.

At this school, perhaps unlike how the incident would have been determined at Feldspar, students noted that, 'In the end it was the principal's choice, in the end, the end thing is the principal is the one that says "Luke, you're going to stay at this school or Luke sorry we can't have you"'. However, he added: 'He is influenced by the students.' The same group of students that told us this story also wanted us to know that not every incident of bad behaviour, or even violence, led to a person being asked to leave. They told us another story of a student on camp who had punched another boy during a card game. In this instance:

> This person felt like it was just a big thing and there was a huge meeting about it. This person didn't get kicked out of the school, he didn't leave the school . . . But that got resolved within the whole school meeting on camp, that actually, like, people talked about it, people talked about the situation, people talked about the context, you know?

One boy talked of the surprise he felt when he was critiqued at a meeting:

> Tyler: I talk a lot in meetings about situations and stuff and then it turned out, without me knowing, that I didn't let a lot of the other people talk and I interrupted a lot what they said, and when this person brought it up I was really like 'Oh no, she's saying I'm a bad person' and then, but like she wasn't, she was just saying like 'I need to bring it up', I really felt like an attack because she didn't bring it up with me before, she didn't say to me beforehand, 'Hey you need to kind of make sure these other people can talk.'

When asked what roles teachers played in these meetings, students indicated that they did have some influence and that people listened to them. There were also instances noted where 'favourite' teachers could have more influence over the meetings than other teachers. However, it was pointed out that: 'There are some teachers which get, like viewed more highly than other[s] but that's also [true] with students.' It was also pointed out to us at Distincta that teachers did not act as mediators in tense situations. Instead we were told, 'We do have mediators which run the meeting, which are students.'

Whilst there was no clear veto structure at Distincta in the same way that existed at St Ebenezer, there was a strong sense that the principal did have the last word on a range of important matters. This was not necessarily regarded as a problem. One former student, now teaching at the school, explained the situation to us:

> He has the final say on everything not because that's necessarily the way he wants it to be, but because, you know everybody is aware that there've been times when the school has been going in a direction that Don is thinking isn't what he had planned and he's stepped in and he's done something about it. And I feel like – and I think that's a good thing because there is, you know you have this one individual who's kind of leading the school which, you know it's tyranny under the illusion of democracy – because everybody has a say but it's really, when it comes down to it Don is making these final decisions because he has to – but I think it's because he has such a clear vision or he has an idea of what is ideal and he can never reach that but he's always working towards it.

The extent to which Distincta was prepared to take the risk with students and key decisions appeared to be less than was the case at Feldspar. At Feldspar it was emphasized over and over to us that teachers had no right of veto in regard to any decision. One aspect of Feldspar, for example, that was very different from many of the other practices in the other sites, and from more mainstream schools, was that the students played a central role in the selection and employment of teachers. This appeared to impact positively upon the teacher–student relationship, for instance, Paige noted that: 'I found that at my old school I wouldn't want to go to some lessons because I didn't like the teacher but here it's just, all the teachers are really nice because everybody's agreed to have them.'

It was at a whole school meeting where decisions about the employment of teachers were made. Teachers were invited to have a trial for a week, both for them to see if they liked the school and for the members of the school community to work out who was suitable for the school. During one of our visits the school was in the process of selecting a new IT teacher. One of the students we interviewed, Riley, explained the process of selecting a teacher and of the rationale that usually underpinned his decision to vote for a particular teacher:

> So at the moment we've got three IT teachers kind of wandering around being on their best behaviour trying to charm us so that we want them in our school (laughs) . . . We employed an IT teacher who wasn't very good

and he generated a lot of resentment, but one of the things I think that people have learnt from that is [about the need for] kind of involvement in the school and going to school meetings and things like that because it's *really* important that the teacher cares about the school a lot. And I think that's actually one of the main things we look for and then of course we do look for academic prowess and actually being able to *teach*. So we have trial lessons with them and, yeah but I think if a student isn't taking part in the lesson they still vote on the teacher because they expect them to become a part of the school. Like, I talk to teachers who don't teach me and I know them very well so, yeah I think, so that's one of the most important things.

Building a democratic community can involve significant work and is not always smooth sailing for the teachers or the students. Sometimes the responsibility that comes with making significant decisions, for example, about the employment of teachers or the enrolment of students can take its toll on students. We were told of one incident at Feldspar where a teacher had been asked to leave by the school meeting. The school had required a new science teacher and they had had only one applicant for the job. After this teacher had been interviewed a large number of students had raised concerns about him, but, as we were told, the school was in desperate need of a science teacher so 'it was sort of shoehorned through probably by adults, by members of the staff more than anything'. When the students started to complain about his ability to communicate and his lack of understanding of the Feldspar culture, the teachers tried to assist:

> After a term or so we said, 'Right, look we as staff we'll sit down and talk with him and we'll try and help him through' and the school meeting said, 'Okay, yes, good let's give him another chance, we'll give him till Easter and reassess.' Come Easter a lot of people felt that the situation hadn't been improved and he ended up being asked to resign and it was just such a long drawn out and painful, painful experience.

This pain was also felt by the students. The teacher went on to say:

> I remember the final meeting which I think lasted about two or three days, because he was very emotional; he loved the school and he was in the school meeting and he was in tears and it was 'please' you know 'I can change' and I remember after the final meeting when he finally offered his resignation, a couple of kids coming to us and going, 'sometimes I just wish someone would make the decisions for us'. So, you know, there is a responsibility in a sense, and it's difficult – it's not easy!

There were a number of other issues that surfaced around the meeting. For instance, some of the students at the schools were not as committed to the meeting process as others. Given that meetings were not compulsory this could cause some meetings to have a low attendance, although when a topic of great interest to the students was to be raised this could increase participation levels. As one teacher, Ian, told us:

> Most kids will look at the agenda and if there's something on like, usually involving a particular computer game (laughs) that someone wants banning because it's overtaking rooms or whatever then they'll go and they'll lobby – but of course the people that attend more regularly are more politically savvy.

Sometimes there were tensions between teachers about process. We were told about one instance of conflict at Feldspar by the two teachers involved. When new students wanted to come to the school they had been interviewed by students and teachers and some concerns had been raised about how much time this had been taking out of lessons. So a new process was initiated whereby much of the information about how the school worked was to be provided to new students in written form. One of the teachers who had been involved in preparing this document put in a sentence which appeared to conflict with the ethos of the school. This teacher explained to us:

> Rita: So although everything is controlled by the meeting they choose not to control everything I suppose is what it's down to. They couldn't do all the finances, the finances particularly, but they have an overview.

As a consequence of this, Rita wrote a sentence in the documentation that said: '*almost* all decisions have to be agreed by the school meeting'. Another teacher, Ian, took exception to the word 'almost' despite recognizing that 'her argument was good' and that they did give a lot of authority to the registrar on financial matters and that the teachers had a lot of say over curriculum matters. However, he saw it as 'a political issue' and thus raised it at a meeting. He told us:

> I wanted to try and get people to care. But I was basically told, 'We don't. The school meeting doesn't want to discuss this' so, 'Yeah we can see that there is a potential problem but' it was like 'You go and fix it' well you and a group of others. So I worried about that because it wasn't even, 'You go and fix it and then bring it back to the school meeting' it was, 'We trust you to go and fix it' . . . They're quite happy and they do trust us, which they're right to and a lot of the way the school works is based on trust, but I don't know for me it's a bit of an un, it's an unsafe, it's a bit too woolly.

Thus, whilst valuing student voice, the three schools had very different 'democratic' structures. St Ebenezer relied on a consensus model whereby decisions could take a long time to make as proposals worked their way through the council processes to the whole school meetings, where silence would be used to wait for a consensus to be reached. There were also some decisions that were made by teachers and by the school executive, although all of these could be challenged through the council system. However, whilst very rarely used, the headteacher did have the power to veto any decision that was made through the school council. Distincta College worked with a premise of 'no rules', where it was suggested that absolutes formed the basis of tyranny. There were regular meetings at the school during which students could raise issues that they were concerned about. These might relate, for instance, to other students, to teachers, to curriculum, to assessment, to the enrolment of students and to the employment of teachers. Every decision that was made at these meetings was always up for review. However, as with St Ebenezer, the principal could veto decisions. In the case of Distincta, the principal had a high degree of ownership of the school, having been the main driver behind its creation. The school had in the past been through some difficult times when there had been conflict between teachers and the school had nearly closed. This right to veto was seen by many within the school as legitimate in the sense that it was seen as necessary to prevent tyranny being created through democracy. Feldspar was prepared to take this risk. The school meeting at Feldspar was the primary decision-making body over which nobody had veto rights. Not every action had to go through the school meeting, but every action could be challenged through it. All key decisions were made at the meeting. We discuss Feldspar in much greater detail in Chapter 6 when we consider issues of representational justice (Fraser 2010).

Making a difference

Biesta's (2007) claim that part of a democratic education was also taking responsibility for the world was evident at both Feldspar and St Ebenezer. At Feldspar, students often travelled in relation to the political work that they were doing as a democratic school. The school was a member of both the International Democratic Education Network (IDEN) and of EUDEC and both teachers and students regularly participated in the International Democratic Education Conference. As part of their political work with these organizations teachers regularly gave talks on democratic education at various venues. One teacher told us how she saw attempts to make education better for all children as an important component of their work. She went on to say:

> Ava: It's the work of members of staff like myself, like, Ian particularly who are very much evangelically going around telling people about what we do and saying, 'You know what? You can do it differently' and, 'You don't have to be scared by us, we don't want you to turn into us but we want you to be aware of this is how we do it' and we find a lot of opposition to that. But on the whole we find a lot of people that are very interested in acknowledging the difference that is around.

Ava was one of the younger teachers at the school and recognized that the local community of the school aided in its success, but was confident that democratic education was not just for middle-class students. She told us:

> I'd love at some point to take this idea, adapt it and put it into Brixton, put it into inner city London where there's forty different languages spoken in the class – somewhere where alternative education isn't such a thing – that would be a huge challenge.

This passion for democratic education was also present in many of the comments that the students were making to us. Jade explained to us how when she came to the school she really had not thought much about education at all. It was just something that somebody did. However, she had become passionate about education as a consequence of attending Feldspar. She told us: 'I didn't realize how important it was but now I think it is *the* be all and end all of everything.' A number of students were active with EUDEC and often went on speaking engagements and visited other democratic or 'progressive schools' for the purposes of learning from them. Jade had been on the council of EUDEC for two years and at the time of our visits had moved on to EUDEC's 'oversight committee', which she told us, 'Is like governors so that you make sure that the council are doing what they say they should, basically.' She was extremely grateful for the experiences that this had given her:

> I don't come from a sort of wealthy background, and up until I came and got involved with EUDEC stuff, I think I'd only been like abroad about two times and in the last few years I've been like all across Europe. I've met loads of people [and] I've got loads of contacts and I did lectures in Croatia and stuff.

Many of the lectures given by the students had been in teacher training institutions, including in Croatia:

> Yeah in Rijeka and it was really exciting because, you know they've all read about Summerhill and then they see real democratic students and they're like 'Oh how exciting' (laughs) . . . I just wanted everybody to have the opportunity that I had, and I now strongly believe that this is the best form of education that there is (slight laugh) but, I'm waiting to be proven wrong, I always like to be proven wrong (laughs).

At the time of one of our visits to the schools some students had recently returned from a democratic schools conference in Copenhagen. Interestingly, attendance at these conferences can lead to students being critical of their own school. One student, Riley, had been very impressed by one school he had visited and come to know there. He described this Danish school as 'one of the best schools in the country' and as 'a really amazing school'. He told us, 'It's very different to here, it's big and there's graffiti everywhere.' He went on to say that students who went to that school did so because they wanted to be political whereas at Feldspar 'people come a lot I think for safety and things like that – it's more of a haven'. For 15-year-old Riley it was disappointing that Feldspar was not more 'political' or 'activist'. When asked whether he meant political in relation to education, he told us:

> Around education but around, like, the war in Iraq, I mean, [at] the school in Copenhagen a lot of the students were going to a march to shut a power plant down. But the school didn't tell them to do that . . . there were just lots of, like, people who really cared about what was going on in the world. And I think here it's not like 'as encouraged'. There I think . . . it was a school which was definitely one of the, it was the best school for studying politics and Copenhagens (sic) would say that; so people went there because they wanted to do things like that. But I don't know, the people just don't seem to care as much here and I don't think it's like, ingrained in the school system to be political.

The ethos of St Ebenezer, whilst not reflecting the politics that would have suited Riley, was very much framed around being part of a global community and recognizing that with that membership comes responsibilities. Adrian, who was head of languages and in charge of a range of activities and had been at the school for 28 years, described the ethos in the following way:

> It's difficult to put the finger on but, the individual is important, *hugely* important, but the individual is nothing unless the individual realizes his or her responsibility to the group, and the group in the twenty-first century is the globe as a human community that shares limited resources.

At the time of our visit the school was involved in global community projects, two in India and one in Kosovo. These projects were part of the senior school's community service requirement. The headteacher, Robert, stressed that this was not a charity exercise. He explained to us:

> What you have to do if you're, for example, if you want to go and work in our summer school in Kosovo which looks after orphans of the genocide there, then you have to develop a skill here, so that might be an art-based skill, a performance-based skill or teaching literacy or advising on women's health issues or whatever. You develop that skill here, then you have to go somewhere locally to practice it, that might be a special school, a homeless shelter, something like that, and then when you've done that, perfected your teaching of it, then you're allowed to go to Kosovo to take part and to share that skill there. So it's very important, you know it's a personal development, it has a local impact and then it has a global impact. And those three things are very important.

The Indian project had begun in 1990 and students from the school have been going back every year since. The guidelines for the project were established early on; the key one, according to a teacher, Adrian, was that it had to operate on the basis of mutual benefit. He indicated that there were obvious benefits to the students and the teachers from St Ebenezer who participated in it.

> For a young person from here or a member of staff from here goes to India, we benefit because it just explodes out of our eyes, you know even after, God knows I've been 15 or so times (laughs) to India in the last 10 or 12 years, but you know every time there's still something new, there's still something that you feel, 'Oh that's really been important.'

However, there had been a commitment to making sure that the project was not just about tourism or short-term charity work. The school liaises closely with various Non-governmental Organizations (NGOs) to undertake work that is perceived to make a real difference to the communities they visit. Adrian went on to explain that the Rajasthan project was part of a broader community development programme. The aspect of the programme where they felt they could help was in a 'learning camp'. This camp brought young people aged 6 to 14 who had never been to school from remote villages to give them an education in basic literacy and numeracy. The students from St Ebenezer were expected to add to this programme through providing simple science experiments. Prior to attending the camp, the St Ebenezer students had to come up with ideas for the experiments and to develop materials for their lessons. The students were told, 'It's no good trying to do experiments there which can't be replicated', for, as Adrian informed us, the Indian teachers in the programme often took on board many of these ideas for their own teaching (some of them later visited St Ebenezer). In addition to going to India the students organized fundraising at home in order to buy materials that could not be accessed in India. Adrian indicated 'this is a project which informs the whole school'. He went on to say how after each visit there was an assembly where students reported back to the whole school and that 'the impression or feeling that is really given is – we're part of our global community, we can learn from each other'. One of the students, Giuseppe from year 12, told us that his trip to India, where 'We went and we helped in a local school there for a few days and experienced their culture and talked about that and then we went on an eleven-day trek' had been the 'best thing about school'.

Conclusion

As part of identifying schools for this research we visited a range of schools working within a democratic framework, including, as we indicated earlier, Summerhill (Neill 1970). Such schools are often characterized as places where little work is done, and where student achievements can be attributed to the middle-class background and cultural capital of the young people (see Stronach and Piper 2009 for discussion of this representation of Summerhill). However, as with our impression of Summerhill, we saw young people at these schools exercising freedom and responsibility in an environment where they engaged actively in the curriculum and sought out academic challenges. For many of these students it was the first time that they had been so engaged. Students at the schools were highly committed to their school. Many made significantly long journeys to come to school and were highly positive about their schools and their teachers.

The students who attended came from varied circumstances; not all were from wealthy, middle-class backgrounds. Many were. However, there were also significant numbers for whom this was not the case and they were only able to attend because of scholarships or fee waivers. There were many students in these schools who had had negative experiences at other schools either as a result of bullying by other students or as a consequence of tensions with teachers and administrators. These schools offered a refuge from such environments. There were also students in all locations for whom the decision to attend their school had been made on the basis of the underpinning politics that valued and acted upon student voice. There was a sense in all schools that the students felt that what they thought mattered to the teachers and to other students and that the structures existed for them to influence decisions.

Within these schools, therefore, democracy was learnt by doing. There was not an assumption that these young people could take on the decontextualized knowledge about what it means to be a citizen to be used beyond school. The schools were concerned with the students as current citizens, not just as future ones. As such, they advocate a purpose of schooling beyond the delivery of curriculum and the pursuit of academic achievement. They suggest that whilst schools do have as one of their significant purposes the promotion of academic engagement and learning, they also need to do more than this (Delpit 2006; Hayes *et al.* 2006). These purposes include playing a part in the creation of and building a commitment to democracy. Indeed one of the reasons behind the setting up of Summerhill was a concern about the growing authoritarianism and fascism in Europe following the First World War. What these schools demonstrate is that schools are political organizations and that the way in which they are organized has implications for the way in which young people learn how to be active citizens.

We are not suggesting that any of these schools reflects a perfect model of democratic education. Each of these schools is faced with its own set of problems which can inhibit democracy and which can lead to tensions between teachers, between students and between students and teachers. Indeed, we claim in Chapter 6 that schools like the ones here need to go beyond a concern with what Fraser (2010) would term representation, or opportunities to make one's voice heard, to be considered democratic in a social justice sense. However, each in its own way provides an example of the dynamic tensions that exist in promoting a democratic form of governance. Thus in foregrounding the work of these schools, what we hope, as Fielding indicates in his research on school meetings in government schools, is that:

> When we actually encounter radical alternatives it is in large part their brute reality, their enacted denial of injustice and inhumanity and their capacity to live out a more fulfilling, more generous view of human flourishing that in turn moves us to think and act differently.
>
> (Fielding 2013, p. 125)

We suggest that the schools in this chapter certainly provide some radical alternatives and clearly demonstrate what is possible when there are organizational forms that are not based on deficit assumptions about young people's capacities to make responsible and informed decisions about their own education. As Ruby from Distincta explained to us, working within an organizational framework based on freedom also taught responsibility:

> It kind of makes you grow up a little bit, having that kind of freedom over your own education which although it may not feel like it in when you're in year 7, 8 and 9 possibly even 10. Once you get older you realize it's actually quite important and, you know, other people at other schools have their, like, have their life totally controlled and we have almost full freedom. And it's something that really falls onto you to kind of grow up and to think of your priorities, really, think of exactly what it is you want to do.

As with the previous chapter, the students in these schools demonstrate the capacities of young people to take control of their own education when treated with respect and when the structures are put in place for them to contribute to major decisions affecting them. In the following chapter we consider some of the experiences of teachers working in both flexible learning centres and democratic schools.

5   Teaching in 'the margins'

We were drawn to the field of alternative education by our concern for the young people who seemed to constitute what Bauman (2011) would call the 'collateral damage' of the neo-liberal paradigm of schooling. However, as the research progressed, we became increasingly interested in the experiences of the teachers and workers who staffed alternative schools. Here it must be noted that in the flexible learning centres, the different roles of teachers and support staff such as youth workers, for example, were not always noted by the students. In the often intense conditions created by caring for and educating young people with high needs, workers and teachers operated side by side responding to the immediate demands of each situation, whether that be by delivering pastoral care or educational support. What mattered to the young people was the relationship, not the role. 'Workers' included a range of people from a variety of professional backgrounds, for example: community service, social work and youth work; along with volunteers from all walks of life. They were drawn to the alternative education sites out of a sense of concern for young people, particularly those who had few resources and/or adult supporters in their lives. Such workers would likely have used their talents wherever there was a need for them in respect to assisting young people; they were not in the alternative sites because they were questioning and/or rejecting the current paradigm of their profession. However, this was certainly the case for the teachers who participated in this research.

Their stories revealed varying levels of disillusionment, dissatisfaction and disappointment with mainstream schooling systems. Their frustrations with what they saw as the increasing demands of educational bureaucracies are summed up in such comments as:

> Neil (Woodlands): I don't have a problem with the students [in mainstream schools]) – it's just the *structures* and it seems to be getting more and *more* structured all the time – new pieces of paper to fill in and a box to tick and a new policy to implement . . .

And this:

> Hugh (St Ebenezer): I moved from the state sector – I was getting very, very frustrated with the exam board and the exams that we had to put the

kids through because it wasn't educational it was just preparing for these blessed modules – hoop-jumping exercises and the real chemistry was going out the window, and I'm very passionate about it!

One of the staff we spoke to at Distincta College was a pre-service teacher who was completing her final professional placement. Caitlin also dreaded the perceived bureaucracy of mainstream schools. When we asked her if she was excited about the prospect of teaching, she replied:

> No, if I was to teach in a place like this I would, but I'm *so* just overwhelmed and put off by the government sort of coming down on schools and all the accountability. It just – it takes away from the professionalism of it, that . . . you're a professional with, you know, years of experience and knowledge in your area of expertise . . . I'd *love* to work in an environment like this because it's sort of put the teaching back into teaching . . . One of the things that turns me off the most about teaching is all the bureaucratic bullshit and it just seems to sort of suck out the passion and the energy of being a teacher, because your energy's being put elsewhere.

The frequency of such comments from teachers in the alternative schools in both the UK and Australia led us to explore more deeply the connections between their disillusionment with mainstream schooling and the current context of educational policies. Thus, whilst in the preceding chapters we explored some of the major impulses of contemporary schooling and their impact upon young people, in this chapter we turn our attention to the teachers we met at the research sites. Here we explore their motivations and teaching philosophies; their frustrations and success stories; their willingness to work in alternative education despite in some cases job insecurity and lower salaries; and their perspectives on the strengths and weaknesses of the alternative sector. We also present the views of staff who came from a non-teaching background. Whilst their reasons for being in the sites were different from those of the teachers, their experiences of working in the sites clearly supported the perspectives of the teachers. For the purposes of this chapter, the term 'worker' is used for staff with a non-teaching background. However, before we turn to the data, it is necessary to look more closely at some of the theoretical debates around the work of teachers.

Contemporary teaching contexts

As globalization fashions national conditions of economic restructuring, labour insecurity and the need for increasing amounts of training/retraining and academic credentialing, the significance of youth attainment in education has taken on a new importance for governments, particularly in the developed North. The 'knowledge economy' (Dolfsma and Soete 2006) of such nations requires educational capital and highly skilled workers to fuel national prosperity and increase international competitiveness. Thus, as we indicated in Chapter 2, the need for the retention of students to senior high school and beyond has become an international priority (OECD 2011). We contend that if such goals are to be reached, we must reaffirm the significance of the teacher–student relationship, the 'care' factor and emotional labour of teachers (Isenbarger and Zembylas 2006). This means also taking into account the levels of satisfaction teachers have with their work.

Teachers are at the centre of the education of young people. Among many variables, much research claims that it is teachers who are the ones who can actually 'make a difference' in the lives of young people (Darling-Hammond 2000; Hattie 2003; King Rice 2003; OECD 2005; Stronge 2007). Although care is needed here, as Hayes *et al.* (2006) argue, teachers do make *a* difference, an important one, but they do not make *the* difference. Such suggestions can work to blame teachers for problems that require significant social policy solutions related to addressing widespread economic and cultural injustices. However, a failure to work with teachers to address the ways in which the needs of their students can be met will do little to improve the quality of pedagogies in schools. As Connell (1994), more than a decade ago, argued 'we cannot ignore them [teachers]. Education as a cultural enterprise is constituted in and through their labour' (p. 138). However, in research from the last two decades (see for example, Connell 1994; Apple 1995, 2000; Smyth *et al.* 2000; Kincheloe 2008), a progressive 'de-skilling' of teachers has been raised as a matter for concern. Similarly, when it comes to the formulation of educational policy the voices of teachers are usually absent. Since the early 1990s, in nations of the Global North, there has been a commensurate change in the modes of accountability demanded from teachers. The establishment of various professional and regulatory bodies have been central to these changes. Perryman describes the situation in England thus:

> Teachers are now accountable through formal audits of student learning outcomes controlled by senior management. Teaching is controlled by the National Curriculum and a performance framework that is backed up by performance management and target-setting. Evidence about performance is based on pupil outcomes, classroom observation and personal statements. Pupils become objects and targets and the headteacher and senior management team are publicly accountable.
>
> (2006, p. 149)

School inspections by the Office for Standards in Education (Ofsted) monitor school standards and progress according to set criteria that echo the regimes of efficiency, productivity, performativity and 'normalization' favoured by neo-liberalism. Deviation from these requirements may be deemed as relevant to school 'failure' (Perryman 2006). Since 2005, the *Inspection Framework* in England has also incorporated more evidence-gathering and self-policing by individual schools. It is not our intention to argue that schools should not meet standards. It is the homogenizing effect of current modes of accountability that we see as detrimental to socially just schooling. 'Outstanding schools' are often seen to be synonymous with a particular model of schooling based on middle-class expectations. Schools that attempt innovative responses to the needs of students whose lives have been shaped by poverty, unemployment and social deprivation, risk government intervention. Schools, and the teachers within them, are disciplined into conformity by 'surveillance, and with it, normalization . . . one of the great instruments of power' (Foucault 1977a, p. 184). For teachers, who may be inspired by individual philosophies of alternative, perhaps democratic paradigms of education, such 'panoptic' (Foucault 1977a) controls are likely to prove challenging at best, and, at worst, lead to considerable personal stress. To varying timelines, similar accountability measures have been underway in the US and Australia.

In the US, states have instituted rewards and 'punishments' for school performances since the 1990s. In 2001, the No Child Left Behind Act (US Department of Education 2001) extended such measures nationally. Recently, interest has shifted towards making the rewards and punishments relevant to individual teacher performances (Rothstein *et al.* 2009). In Australia, the debates around teacher performance pay have culminated in the release of an *Australian Teacher Performance and Development Framework*, developed by the Australian Institute for Teaching and School Leadership (AITSL 2012). Under this proposal teachers set performance goals every year and are expected to demonstrate how those goals have been met. Evidence to support teacher performance includes: student results, feedback from students, parents, peers and/or supervisors along with classroom observations of their teaching. In 2012, the current Australian Commonwealth Minister for School Education announced new accountability measures for teachers. As reported in the *Sydney Morning Herald*:

> Every school teacher faces an annual performance review with education ministers set today to approve a national framework for assessments to begin next year. The actual form of the review will be left to individual schools and school systems but the ministers will commit to begin the process of reviewing the work of the country's 290,000 teachers. Reviews will be led by the principal, a senior teacher or an outsider could be brought in. They are expected to include observation of classroom performance, student results and feedback from both parents and students . . . Teachers will be given a set of documented, measurable and specific goals that will be agreed with their school principal or a delegate.
>
> (*Sydney Morning Herald*, 3 August 2012)

Whilst we acknowledge the need for a skilled teaching workforce, such account-ability measures run the risk of validating and rewarding teaching practices that conform to a traditional, hierarchical, industrial model based on measurable inputs and outcomes; and a disciplined student populace acquiring the necessary skills to be valued members of the marketplace: the required 'human capital' of the neo-liberal vision of society. Indeed, we argue that there is much that cannot be 'measured' when it comes to assessing the outcomes of an education (see for example, Delpit 2006). The complexities of the teaching and learning relationship between instructors and their pupils include an emotional, relational element (Noddings 1996) that is fundamental to educational labour and the retention of young people in learning. The lives of many young people are shaped by the debilitating effects of poverty and a myriad of marginalizing intersecting sociocultural factors of 'difference' that may include gender, race, class, ethnicity and religion along with a range of physical and cognitive conditions (see for example, Connell 1993; Apple 2010; Ritter and Lampkin 2012). Many such students begin their education without the necessary skills and/or cultural capital (Bourdieu 1984) to connect with their schools emotionally and to succeed academically. Many lack social networks of support from families, community groups and other guiding adult influences. For such young people, the school and the people within it become crucial funds of the social, emotional and educational capital they need for their future well-being (Croninger and Lee 2001).

Neo-liberalism with its inherently instrumentalist approach has seen Western governments attempt to define the complex act of teaching via sets of professional standards. Within the Australian State of Queensland, as indicated in Chapter 2, attempts to define the work of teachers resulted in 195 individual standards of teaching knowledge, practice and values to which teachers had to adhere and provide evidence of renewing on a yearly basis (Queensland College of Teachers 2006). The new set of national standards being rolled out to replace the State based models in Australia will comprise 42 standards of knowledge, practice and values which will then be further categorized according to whether an individual teacher is assessed at the following level: graduate; proficient; highly accomplished; or lead (AITSL 2013). In her framework for understanding teacher professional identity, Mockler argues that:

> Over the course of a career and mediated by a complex interplay of personal, professional and political dimensions of teachers' lives [professional teacher identity] is infinitely more multifarious than assessments of teachers' work based on 'role' or function such as those inevitably embedded in professional standards.
>
> (2011, p. 518)

She reminds us of Dewey's (1897, p. 80) assertion that teachers are 'engaged, not simply in the training of individuals, but in the formation of the proper social life' (cited in Mockler 2011, p. 518). Thus, current measurement regimes ignore the complexity of teachers' work and consequently undervalue their potential to be significant factors in the retention of young people in education.

Within the literature (see for example, Lortie 1975; Huberman 1993; Alsup 2006; Flores and Day 2006; Beauchamp and Thomas 2009; Cohen 2010), the notion of individual 'teacher identity' is of significant interest and thus must be considered in this discussion. We do not adopt the position that there is one 'desirable' teacher identity nor that identity is fixed for individual teachers. Rather we adopt the postmodern perspective that identity-building is a discursive, reflexive project (see for example, Foucault 1980; Giddens 1991; Hall 1996). In terms of fashioning their professional identity, teachers draw upon their training along with a range of relevant political perspectives, philosophies and lived experiences. Reflective of the general community there will be a range of perspectives that one might plot along a continuum from conservative to radical. In terms of responding to the needs of vulnerable young people it is difficult to predict which personalities and approaches 'work'. We contend that 'successful' teacher–student relationships are highly individualized but nevertheless founded upon some commonalities that draw upon principles of respect, care, honesty, supportiveness and a desire to help young people progress academically, vocationally and socially so as to achieve personal goals. Within the various sites of our research into flexible learning centres and democratic schools, we found many such teaching professionals.

Who works in alternative education?

People have come to work in this educational sector through a variety of pathways. As well as long-term teachers, we came across a former detective, motor mechanics, engineers, social workers, community services personnel and youth workers. Many of the sites were also supported by volunteers (often retirees) and charitable organizations. People had all sorts of varying qualifications: for instance, in addition to teaching qualifications, we found the following mix at The Garage: a Bachelor of Applied Social Science in Counselling and Communication; an Advanced Diploma in Theology; a Certificate of Occupational Studies in Plumbing; a Certificate III in Hospitality, Food and Beverage; and voluntary experience in a counselling service for people with depression. For both teachers and workers, in a number of sites, the job was emotionally stressful due to the difficult life circumstances of the students; there were also stresses in terms of job security and working conditions. For many of these people the stresses, uncertainties and lower pay were a trade-off they were prepared to make for being in a job that they regarded as being highly satisfying. It was not uncommon to find workers and teachers emphasizing how much they enjoyed working with the young people. At The Garage, Charles, a former motor mechanic, now teacher and guidance officer, stated that: 'I love what I do. This is probably the most satisfying job . . . the most stressful.' Wayne, also from The Garage, commented that he felt most satisfied when he could see that the young people enjoyed what they did and felt proud of their achievements: 'You give them some tools . . . and they do it and they feel really good about themselves.' This satisfaction came about for a number of reasons. However, central to these reasons was the sense that they were really making a difference to young people's lives, especially to those who had difficult lives. For example, reflective of the philosophy of the staff at The Garage as well as a number of other sites visited, one of the workers proudly commented, 'We catch the kids that have fallen through the fingers of society.' For the non-teaching staff, the alternative sites (usually the flexi schools) provided them with opportunities to enact their commitment to young people and the 'common good'.

Additionally, many of the workers in these sites came to the sector out of a personal mission to make schooling better for young people who were like them. It was not uncommon for us to come across such personnel who had also had bad schooling and/or difficult life experiences and who were thus enthusiastic about supporting young people facing similar challenges. For instance, Charles from The Garage described how he responded to the young people who asked what he would know about their lives:

> I said, 'But I was one of you guys' . . . I was homeless; I was a rat bag, got into a lot of trouble, grew up, came to live in Queensland with an older brother and met my wife. That's probably the easiest way to say it. I've told them that I was homeless, how I worked to support myself from 14 and that. I don't know if they believe me but I can see what they're doing.

It was often the case that the salaries of the teaching staff were significantly lower than those received by their peers in the more regulated mainstream schools. However, for teachers, engaging in alternative education was often a political decision. Woodlands Flexi School was run under the auspices of a local high school; Rhys, a teacher at that high school, had volunteered to take up a position at the Flexi School based on his attraction to the politics found in the 1970s' ideas of alternative education and his commitment to democratic forms of schooling. Workers at Victoria Meadows Flexi School were driven by their commitment to developing community. The commitment of an Indigenous teacher, Kathy, at Fernvale Education Centre was shaped by her experiences of and desire to challenge racism:

> As a Murri[1] person . . . I hear the horror stories out there about kids going into classrooms . . . and *I* was one of those kids . . . Even at university, when I was sitting in a big lecture theatre I had one of my fellow students get up and say, 'Well if I had my way I would have shot a lot of the Black bastards years ago' – they were her words not mine. And you know and it's scary to think that this person's going to go out there to be a teacher.

Throughout this chapter we have selected data from teachers and principals/ school managers from both the flexible learning centres and the democratic schools. The quotations from staff have been selected according to their capacity to best represent common ideas and core themes contained within the data from across the various sites. One of the key people within all sites was the headteacher, principal or manager, who was often the person who had been responsible for, or highly influential in, the school's/centre's foundation. However, such positions were not without their challenges. We begin our analysis of our data with such administrators of flexible learning centres and democratic schools.

Teaching in alternative schools

Being an administrator of an alternative school seems to be a job that takes its toll. It was not uncommon to find that such personnel were on extended sick leave. However, this job was nevertheless a source of great personal satisfaction to these people as opposed to the stress of the mainstream. The principal and founder of one such school stated:

> Don (Distincta College): 'Why did I start?' . . . I get such a buzz out of kids turning around . . . I wanted to get into an environment where I could teach my way without interference. I just needed not to fight against the system constantly . . . I was starting to stress out, have heart attack symptoms.

However, it was clear that both he and his staff had been through some challenging times in respect to financing the school:

> Our funding is gradually improving but every once in a while we have some horrible glitch . . . If we ever need money the *only* way that money comes is out of my pocket *or* the teachers have to take no pay . . . and they have mortgages to pay . . . I went to the point of near personal bankruptcy . . . I was desperately hanging on to the last straw – every bit of it as I could – and managed to make it work.

One of the first contentious issues raised by principals, headteachers and managers related to the questionable usefulness of national testing regimes currently favoured by many educational authorities to measure academic progress. For example, the headteacher of St Ebenezer, Robert, had this to say about the English SATs:

> *You don't do them?*
> No, no, absolutely nonsense. All they do is compare one child with another which is ridiculous! You can opt out of the things like the *Sunday Times* league table. The government league tables you can't opt out of, but we've opted out of *everything* we can . . . If you want to know how a child is doing, then ask their teacher. And the teacher, if they don't know, they shouldn't be teaching!

Like the UK, Australia employs a testing regime similar to SATs, NAPLAN. The teachers and administrators of the Australian alternative schools expressed a similar disdain for these processes:

> *What about when NAPLAN time comes around, how does the school engage with that?*
> Anna (Distincta College): We don't prep the kids, it is just about who they are, and I don't, I kind of would feel a bit sad if we have to prep them

(big sigh) – bit counter-productive or something, I don't know . . . But, I know with the, like, the importance of 'looking good', yeah it makes a difference to the school, but I don't think it makes a difference in that we now need to train to the NAPLAN.

As a registered school, Victoria Meadows was subject to the same testing regimes as all other Australian schools. This had led to some discussion about whether or not the government funding that they received as a school was worth the constraints that accompanied it. John, the 'principal' of Victoria Meadows, was very passionate about this issue and objected to the discourses inherent in the name 'school' and the various terms coined to describe attempts to provide 'alternative' modes of education:

John: When you say 'alternative school' it means, 'Oh we had schools and they're fine and teaching's fine but we had to make something different for *you* because *you* obviously don't fit!' I think the answer is not *school* . . . we're playing the game called 'school'. What we need to be is *not* be a bloody school! . . . I don't call this place a school. I call it a community, a learning community . . . To me this place is a community – it's a community with a particular focus – *learning*.

Such administrative attitudes were common among the school principals, headteachers and managers whom we met and they resonated with the dissatisfaction felt by classroom teachers who went looking for alternative career pathways. As noted by Ian from Feldspar:

It happened by pure serendipity really. I think a lot of people who go into teaching go in with kind of very idealistic ideas about sort of wanting to pass on skills and there's an element of wanting to help and improve people's future and all of that sort of stuff so I went in with those ideals [and] very quickly found that the teaching profession certainly in the state sector didn't really lend itself very well to that cooperative sort of socialist-type, type ethos and that actually it was about asserting authority, and I couldn't, just because of the way my personality had developed . . . So of course the kids weren't going to [listen], no matter how much I worked at it.

Elaborating on such perspectives, the discussion that follows is structured around three sub-themes that emerged from our interviews with staff: teaching philosophy; school environment; and professional freedom.

Teaching philosophy

Throughout the years we have supervised and taught beginning teachers and worked beside and interviewed established teachers; we have heard many stories about why people have chosen teaching as a career. Typically, most teachers express a desire to help young people to learn and to grow. They do not necessarily agree on the best way to achieve that, but most express a commitment to the well-being of their students, not to the production of test scores, and league tables as evidence of systemic 'success'. Indeed, most lecturers who are involved in teacher education encourage pre-service teachers to focus on student-centred strategies that allow for multiple opportunities for achievement and recognition that educating a child involves more than producing numerical grades. However, whilst mainstream schooling authorities seem to agree with this philosophy in their public pronouncements, in practice, the panopticon of the state and its bureaucratic surveillance of teachers (Fuller *et al.* 2008) and testing of students indicate a different agenda; an agenda that has a clear focus on measureable data. The stress-levels of many teachers and their subsequent early burn-out may be attributed to the increasing pressure 'to perform' within schooling contexts grappling with the challenges from socio-economic issues and the behavioural problems of their students. In some cases such conditions have forced teachers to become someone other than who they wanted to be and departure from the system became a matter of personal survival. For example, we were told by one teacher:

> Ian (Feldspar): I taught for a year in a traditional school . . . But I just found it very difficult being in constant opposition to the kids . . . we were told there's almost a rule that they give you at the start and they said, 'Don't smile until Christmas (laughs)!' You know – if you show a sign of weakness they will defeat you and that's the way the system is . . . And, it was everything that I was opposed to and I didn't like it and I couldn't do it.

For other teachers, the escape from the constrictions of state control was a huge relief:

> Lyn (St Ebenezer): I teach English Lit. . . . you've got the freedom to be able to think '*how* do you want to assess, *why* are you assessing?' . . . I think that in this kind of environment that allows you to really look at each individual student, and target setting is not just *number crunching*! It's above and beyond assessment (slight laugh) I think.

The constant evaluation of students' scores and comparison of schools in the mainstream bothered many teachers who were highly critical of the marketization of education:

> Guy (Distincta College): I kind of look at mainstream schools [as] a reflection of a real consumer culture and it really *forces* people to . . . compete and to be a bit nasty with each other and to be very self-centred and I just didn't feel that was a good idea. And so I liked the idea of alternate education where you can engage with individuals . . . and actually get to know them a little bit.

Most of the teachers interviewed for this research adhered strongly to various notions of student voice and democratic schooling. Typical views are as follows:

> George (Victoria Meadows): Many of the structures in mainstream school are hierarchical and power-based or authority-based and that can be sort of a real death knell for trying to build community . . . Community can't be an add-on . . . there's no reason why a community can't be a learning community. It needs to be that the young person is *foremost*, the curriculum is second and that is a big shift which I don't know whether – not just teachers – I don't know whether the education system per se is ready to make that shift – but I live in hope!

Most teachers were pleasantly surprised to find that such schools existed:

> Ian (Feldspar): So I went there [job ads in the paper] and I came across this little ad and it started talking about equality, *equality* between staff and students and straightaway that's what I'd been looking for . . . I went onto the website . . . and what I found was that there were phrases on the Feldspar website at the time that matched almost *word for word* with my philosophy on education!

They revelled in the opportunity to focus on relationship-building as opposed to the constant imposition of rules. Neil from Woodlands Flexi School expressed it this way:

> The [mainstream] focus on telling them to 'pull up your socks' and 'put that away' and 'stop doing that' and 'comb your hair' [would mean] I'm no longer talking to them *about them*, you know? 'What's going on at home?', 'What did you do on the weekend?', or, 'How's your maths going?' And it is just the wrong focus because it *breaks* your relationship with them.

However reinvigorated teachers felt in respect to their professional lives, teachers also worried about the material impact of their employment choices on other areas of their lives. Most had mortgages or rent to pay and families to provide for; they sometimes worried about being able to continue working in the alternative education sector simply because of lower salaries and often tenuous contracts. They also talked frankly about heavy workloads and the emotional demands of their jobs and students who challenged their patience and exhausted their capabilities; however the *joy* they talked of emanating from their work stopped them from leaving:

> Anna (Distincta College): The connectedness, the feeling of being connected to other people and the students so kind of met with my own personal sort of philosophies . . . I was so exhausted that first year of teaching and my head, my brain, was fried and I had a lot of frustrations and whatnot throughout

the day. But driving home I'd always feel the smile muscles (laughs) had been active all day! So I'd go, 'Yep this is really *it*!' Like there're those elements of frustration and exhaustion and self-doubt and all of that kind of stuff but I *still* felt that I was in a place that I really *wanted* to be in.

And

> Guy (Distincta College): For me I feel like I'd *much* rather work at Distincta College and have less pay and have to put a lot more in and do that and at the end of the day go home and feel *satisfied*. You're very tired but feel satisfied – 'Right, yep, that was good today'. Not go home and just think, 'Gee I hate those people I work with, what a terrible administration'.

Interestingly some teachers were uncomfortable with the idea that there was some kind of special 'philosophy' guiding them. Instead they talked about helping to fulfil a range of basic human needs for the young people in their care:

> John (Victoria Meadows): I'm deeply suspicious of ideology and philosophy or in some cases the theology that says we are here for the young people, we are 'client-focused' – I think that's crap. We are here for *each other* and in doing so we will be more effective. And if we don't do this, it goes pear shape because then everybody starts justifying all sorts of dodgy things . . . and you get all this power.

Thus, across the data pertaining to teaching philosophies the following terms occurred over and over: relationships; the student; equality; community; and how these elements facilitated more authentic learning experiences for students. Elaine from West Canal Alternative School summed it up as 'being there for the young person': 'We want them to succeed, kind of thing. I think if you come in straight from the word go and think, "This is just like any other job," you are not going to get West Canal Alternative School.'

Alternative education often suffers an image problem because of assumptions that the curriculum is less rigorous with a focus on vocational and lower-order knowledge and skills. In spite of this, we have found great diversity among alternative schools. Whilst some may well fit that description, there are many others endeavouring to offer a different kind of education – not an inferior one. Academic outcomes were very important at our research schools, but expectations were shaped by concerns for student progress without the imperative to compare one young person with another:

> *What provisions are made for students who aren't performing well academically?*
> Robert (St Ebenezer): Well, it depends what you mean by performing well 'academically' . . . if they're not performing to their *potential* then we need to find out why that is. And that very much depends on their age, because

some of the children go backwards at various stages, you know? And that's absolutely fine as long as you've got a handle on it.

As well as foregrounding such philosophies, teachers also commented on the environment in which they now worked. However, this usually related to the human environment rather than the physical attributes of their schools.

School environment

Our research schools were diverse in terms of their physical environments and levels of material support. St Ebenezer, for example, offered its students many comfortable, well-resourced buildings. This stood in stark contrast to the smallest flexi school (Cave Street) in our study which consisted of a single area under a house. There was a total enrolment of only twenty-one students who had to attend in shifts of seven because of the very small space in which they worked. It was cold in winter and hot in summer and the few computers they had were old, slow and failed to work most of the time. Juliet, the teacher from Cave Street, was employed by the State government through funding from a range of schools that referred their students to the school. She indicated that the conditions were far worse than in other government-funded mainstream schools. She had tried to get senior people to come and see the conditions they were working under:

> Nobody ever visits here. The principal of Gum Tree (one of the main funding schools) has never been here. The Regional Director of Behavioural Support Services, I tried last year to get a visit happening, kept getting lost and I kept getting directed through lower echelons of management . . . So yeah they haven't been here, so they have no idea what the working situation, the working conditions. I mean it wouldn't pass an occupational health and safety down there – and it does get hot in summer we have pedestal fans here. We have to buy a heater for winter. We've only recently had the café blinds put up, prior to that when I first started that was completely open so when the winds of August came, concrete floor except that mat under the table. I don't believe this. I've never taught . . . I would never have done it, it's only because I've become attached to these young people that I haven't bothered to pursue the mainstream.

However, despite the great differences in the physical environment, these schools shared many commonalities in terms of the human environment. George from Victoria Meadows stressed the importance of community in contrast to some structures he had experienced in mainstream schools:

> I think in mainstream school it is the role of the teacher to drive that [educational] agenda and to drag, pull or push young people along with it. And I think that's one of the advantages that Victoria Meadows has is that

it started with community and has introduced education rather than being education and introducing community development.

Also important was the sense of informality and equality demonstrated in the lack of uniforms, the use of first names and the insistence on mutual respect:

> Anna (Distincta College): I think I'd struggle now with meeting all the written expectations [of mainstream schools] I think. I don't have to give a detention here, I don't have to check that they're wearing the right colour knickers . . . that would absolutely do my head in – I just can't make sense of that.

> Elaine (West Canal Alternative School): He calls me 'Miss' [pointing at a student]. But I don't have them call me 'Miss'. I hate it. It makes me sound old. They all call me Elaine. We all have our hoodies on like this. We are kind of on an equal par. I say to myself, 'I am here to teach you. If you are here to learn, I am here to teach. But we are all on an even level. So let's treat each other the same. I'm not going to treat you any different, unless you don't want to play by the rules because we all do.'

And Adrian from St Ebenezer:

> I hate to hark on about it but, you know the lack of uniforms, the referring to teachers by their first names, the relationship between teacher and pupils, self-government system – you see all those things and it's a much more – I think it creates a much more cohesive environment that students can immediately latch on to and really enjoy.

Such egalitarian relationships also facilitated learning in the classrooms we visited because students were able to be open and honest about the success of lessons. For example, Elaine from West Canal Alternative School saw it as positive that the young people could say exactly what they thought:

> If you run a lesson and it's rubbish, they will come up to you and say, 'That lesson was disgusting. I hated it.' And then you know you are not doing your job properly and you think, 'Right, that doesn't work for that group.'

The way people treat each other impacts upon the emotional climate of places and this was frequently noted by our interviewees. For example, Victoria Meadows Flexi School had replaced traditional school rules with the *Four Rs* – rights, respect, relationships and responsibilities. These applied to staff and students alike. In various ways, the other schools affirmed the importance of these elements as summed up by Edward from Distincta College, who said it was a matter of 'treating people as they treat you . . . with a sense of fairness or balance . . . for example, never yell[ing] at the kids; never [being] aggressive towards them and always [being] courteous'. George, from Victoria Meadows, affirmed the need for having:

> a place where difference is accepted, where alternative viewpoints are accepted; alternative lifestyles are accepted in a safe and respectful environment where your ability to succeed in academic endeavours isn't the be all and end all of you as a person.

Another factor that contributed to the positive environment experienced in these schools was the size of the classes, as noted in this exchange:

> *So what do you see as the strengths of the school?*
> Ethan (St Ebenezer): Definitely the low class size, small class size . . . So you *can* be more spontaneous and make the lessons more interesting. So that's, yeah the small class sizes that was the best thing.

St Ebenezer with approximately 500 students was, in fact, the largest of our research schools. Yet it was still able to implement organizational structures that preserved a low staff:student ratio. Enrolments in the other alternative sites in our study were considerably lower and this was also considered one of their strengths. Because of the small enrolments, teachers were able to provide more individualized attention to their students; they could get to know their students in more depth and shape learning pathways specific to the needs of their students.

Here it must be noted that we did not seek to look uncritically at the practices of the schools we visited. Interviews with staff and students were conducted in private and anonymity was guaranteed. Yet what participants said to us consistently, across the various schools, was that these schools were largely 'happy places'. This perspective was summed up very well by Adrian, a teacher at St Ebenezer:

> I think we build [relationships] – I think to me that's why *I'm* happy – you know I could not work in a place where I didn't feel I'd have a good relationship with the people I work with. We actually treat every individual as an individual.

In terms of shaping these 'happy places', there was a necessary ingredient that teachers identified as vital to making the alternative schools different from mainstream schools. That ingredient was freedom.

Professional freedom

During the post-Cold War decades, global capitalism and its inherent market mechanisms of competition and accountability have increasingly influenced education systems. Such processes have often served to de-professionalize headteachers and teachers, stripping them of the power to make many school-based decisions for their students (Maguire and Pratt-Adams 2009). This can be seen both in the development of national curricula and national and international standardized tests. A key motive driving some of our participating teachers to work in alternative schools was the desire to take back control of what and how they taught in their classrooms:

> Rose (St Ebenezer): Coming here as a teacher it was the freedom, the not being tied . . . because I started teaching as the national [English] curriculum here came in . . . and it was becoming more and more prescriptive and restrictive really, and so coming here we had a lot more freedom in what to do.

And:

> Philip (Woodlands): I like to have my own free will with my programme . . . As a teacher you're the programme designer as well, and that's the one thing I like. I dread just teaching someone else's programme. I've always been able to teach my own programme and that's one of the best things down here.

When Zane from Distincta College was asked why he was so positive about the school, he replied:

> I tell you the truth – freedom, tell you the truth – freedom, because it's like definitely it's half the salary . . . because it's a relaxed environment, because it's a small class . . . so that's why I like [Distincta] because I don't want to be stressed.

For John, teaching at Victoria Meadows allowed him the freedom to reconceptualize the very notion of school, commenting that, 'It's not surprising I'm here because my interest has been developmental work – work about social change, people [and] empowerment and the whole idea of developing "community" was very exciting.' However, despite the many positives of teaching in alternative schools, staff also alluded to the financial sacrifices that came with working in alternative education. Several teachers commented that it was the conditions, not the young people that made the job less attractive for them. For instance, one teacher, Charles, who had told us how much he enjoyed the job, stated:

> Look, the only thing that . . . is a stickler with me is money. If someone offered me more money I'm afraid I'd go . . . Put it this way, I earn under 50,000 a year. I can walk out of here and . . . get 80,000 a year, and that's the sticking point at the moment because money's tight.

Teachers at the Australian Flexi schools Woodlands and Victoria Meadows, both schools that catered to students who had dropped out or had been expelled from mainstream schools, found the emotional demands particularly challenging:

> Angela (Victoria Meadows): We've got a couple of kids who have like very tentative housing arrangements – so one kid that lost his house a few weeks ago he's sort of in a share house situation and then that fell apart then I don't know he would have been homeless for a little bit and now he's kind of organized a meeting with somebody he knows' family. And another girl she was homeless for quite a while but now she's living with her boyfriend's mum and her boyfriend . . . I reckon one of our big weaknesses is that you know we just, a lot of our young people need one-on-one and we just don't have that ratios, not that you're going to get one-on-one ratios.

And:

> Pauline (Woodlands): We debrief a lot at the end of the day. We do have tough days, we have sad days, we hear sad stories and kids who have been kicked out of home, you know like those sorts of things and you've got to try and find shelter for the night, clothing – things like that. So we do debrief a lot at the end of the day and we do work well as a team and we do talk a lot about our cases.

However, the rewards for such emotional investment were many, as summed up by Elaine from West Canal Alternative School:

> We try and get every pupil to do the Duke of Edinburgh . . . A lot of people didn't want to do it. 'No, it will be cold. It will be horrible.' Some of them have done it. And they did absolutely brilliant . . . I love it when they come back [after they have finished at the school]. They come back – they always make me jump. They bang that window. I'm like . . . 'What do you want?' They won't leave me alone. It's wonderful!

In the independent, fee-paying schools of St Ebenezer, Feldspar and Distincta College, teachers were not faced with many of the problems that come with the homelessness, poverty and alienation of abused and neglected young people. Their challenge revolved around the sustainability of their ethos and financing the material needs of both students and staff. However, subsequent material sacrifices seemed to have been made willingly by the staff. The following comment sums up such perspectives:

> Guy (Distincta College): Pay's awful (laughs), I mean, not as awful as it was, but, I mean, it's not a reflection on the school it's more just the circumstances, you know. Just after I started working here full time in 2003 there were some difficulties. We lost a lot of students, and so numbers went down. I think there was about a six-week period where there was *no* pay and so it was just

like . . . 'Oh I really love this school, what a great idea but (slight laugh) I can't put petrol in my car at the moment!' But despite all of that I like the idea that at the end of a six year period you genuinely feel like you've made a *difference*.

However, this does not mean that there are not issues in terms of retaining staff. In the flexible learning centres where staff had to cope with the needs of young people facing homelessness, abuse, addictions and mental illnesses one teacher noted that 'It takes a very special person, I think, to be able to cope with the high levels of stress that can be placed upon them especially over a period of time.'

Conclusion

Current times are difficult for teachers in places such as England and Australia. The present policy context has led to increasing surveillance of their work, often accompanied by a 'de-professionalization' of their labour, along with increased accountabilities and professional competitiveness. Within this environment, a desire to make a positive difference to the lives of young people, a traditional reason for selecting teaching as an occupation (Lortie 1975; see also Day 2004), is difficult to satisfy. The thwarting of this desire was apparent in many of the interviews we conducted with teachers in alternative education settings.

The primary purpose of our research has been to try to understand the practices in alternative schools that would serve to inform the ways in which students who are disengaged from mainstream schooling might be re-engaged. We expected to meet students who had tales to tell of their disenchantment with the mainstream sector. However, we also met teachers who had become disengaged and disenchanted with the mainstream sector, and we found that such concerns were grounded in a sense of commitment to the well-being of students along with the need to nurture their own professional and emotional well-being. For them there was more at stake than material rewards, as noted here by Anna from democratic, fee-paying Distincta College who commented, 'I needed to let go of the money if I'm making that choice . . . I've lived on a lot less . . . so it was about the *quality of life* for me.' Teachers in the flexible learning centres echoed this view, as noted by Neil from Woodlands who told us:

> I've been out of the mainstream for a little while now . . . and I do go back up there [to the high school that has responsibility for Woodlands] and I look at them in their different environment and the way they deal with students differently. I find that *really* difficult I suppose – the way they switch from being a real person to being a teacher (laughs)!

In the alternative schools considered here, the teachers often did not have the same job security, pay and leave conditions as teachers working in the mainstream sector. However, these teachers were still highly committed to their students and their schools. For many of these teachers the personal satisfaction that came from working in their respective schools more than made up for any loss in conditions. Core to this satisfaction was the alignment between their personal philosophies of education and those of the school; an environment that was free of many of the minor but conflict-provoking irritants often present in mainstream schools; and the professional freedom they were accorded as teachers. This would suggest that in order to address the needs of students marginalized from schooling, there is also a need to address the personal and professional needs of teachers.

The interview data from the teachers in these schools provide an insight into some of the damaging effects of current education policies on teachers. The significance of these data is that these teachers became highly committed to their schools and their students when provided with the opportunity to conduct their work in an environment that focused on the educational, physical and emotional needs of young people; recognized and valued their professional expertise; minimized avenues for conflict between teachers and students; and enabled them to develop both collegial and authentic relationships with co-workers and students through democratic processes. In contemporary times there are policy discourses which seek to enforce this commitment through forms of surveillance. The teacher interview data here would seem to suggest that these discourses are not having their desired effects and that retaining teachers in the profession and promoting greater teacher commitment to schools and to students would benefit from a rethink about both the culture of schooling and the dominance of neo-liberal policy agendas in schools. Taking the lens of Nancy Fraser's (2010) framework for social justice and holding it up to the lives of teachers both in the mainstream and in the alternative education sector, it is clear that many teachers in alternative settings are forced to sacrifice their right to distributive justice by, for example, accepting lower salaries and poorer conditions, because in their professional lives they crave recognitive and representational forms of justice linked to their having a meaningful voice in their schools in respect to significant pedagogical and curricular decisions that cater to individual differences in teaching and learning. For their mainstream counterparts the issue is often the reverse: distributive justice without recognition and representation as teaching professionals. We contend that it is educationally counter-productive for all concerned that such choices are forced upon the very people who are best positioned to make a difference in the lives of our young people. Central to this book is the call for social justice for all who come to our schools: students, workers *and* teachers.

Note

1 The Murri people are the traditional Aboriginal owners of parts of Queensland and Northern New South Wales.

6 Case studies
'Oppositional alternatives'

This chapter is concerned with what the schools considered in this book can contribute to understandings of a socially just education system. To facilitate this analysis, we are working with the same notion as Gale and Densmore (2000), that: 'democracy is a precondition for social justice' (p. 143). In so doing we recognize that socially just schooling seeks to work towards 'parity of participation' (Fraser 2010). Fraser argues that parity of participation in the life of society is affected by injustices grounded in lack of opportunities to contribute meaningfully to the decisions that impact upon one's well-being (representation); by injustices that are based on economic inequalities and lack of material resources (distribution); and by injustices that are formed around discriminatory practices that devalue certain cultural groups (recognition). In this chapter we foreground these particular aspects of social justice being addressed within three of our case study schools. We have sought to demonstrate how each school works to enable young people to obtain parity of participation by challenging particular forms of injustice and through the construction of alternative ways of operating than is the norm in many mainstream schools. Thus, loosely using Nancy Fraser's framework, we consider how different (in)justices are addressed within each of these schools. As we indicated in the introduction to the book, the particular focus here is on schools that in Raymond Williams' (1980) terms could be described as 'oppositional' rather than as simply 'alternative'.

We suggest that these schools are 'oppositional' in that they work to challenge the inequities that serve to marginalize particular groups of young people in and beyond the school. We also contend that whilst some schools pay lip-service to concerns with democracy via, for example, student representative councils, the case studies presented in this chapter all demonstrate a more holistic commitment to democracy in their organizational structure, support services, curricula and pedagogical practices. Additionally, the relationship between democratic education and social justice is demonstrated by these schools' attempts to address inequities beyond the school. It is this relationship which, as Beane and Apple (1999) suggest, distinguishes democratic schools from simply being 'progressive'. We are mindful of the point made by Biesta (2007, p. 744) that 'schools can neither create nor save democracy'. However, we are of the opinion that schools, as important social institutions, have a role to play in challenging inequities beyond the school and in providing young people with opportunities to experience working in an environment that struggles with the everyday complexities of pursuing a social justice agenda.

As Gale and Densmore indicate, democratic education is more than just being about access, or equal opportunity. As they state, 'the skills and dispositions of citizenship are best developed through their free exercise' (2000, p. 86). In this chapter we are thus concerned with the ways in which schools' concerns with democracy intersect with a commitment to socially just practices. Drawing on Nancy Fraser (2010) we contend that democratic schools pursue a social justice agenda aimed towards ensuring that no students are denied the ability to participate meaningfully in society because of their educational experiences. Fraser suggests that such participation requires political representation in the affairs impacting upon one's life, a fair distribution of societies' wealth and resources, and a valuing and recognition of cultural difference. As such, we argue that to deserve the title of 'socially just', schools need to ensure that all those participating in the life of the school are involved in the governance of the school (representation); that young people are not denied access to the school or a quality curriculum as a consequence of material disadvantage (distribution); and that within the school no-one experiences oppression as a result of being 'different' (recognition). However, as we indicated above, we also believe that truly democratic schools go beyond operational issues and also seek to address injustices happening beyond their borders. We thus argue, in line with Gale and Densmore that 'effective teaching from the perspective of (socially) just schooling, requires a continual striving towards extending and enhancing democracy in society, just as it demands the teaching and practice of democratic skills and the adoption of democratic dispositions inside schools' (2000, p. 143).

A key feature of a democratic education system is, as Fielding and Moss (2011) indicate, the 'common school', or a school for *all* people. However, the three case-study schools that we are considering in this chapter are not all 'common' in this way. Whilst two of them enrol many students who have been rejected by mainstream schools, the third is fee-paying. However, we believe it is valid to include both models because they both provide insights into what a common school *could* look like and in different ways address the key elements of democratic education. However, we also acknowledge that within all three schools there are aspects of their practices which work against socially just schooling. We indicate some of these tensions at the end of this chapter.

The schools

In this chapter we draw on data from three very different schools. At the time of our visits, as now, they aspire to forms of democratic governance. One of these is a fee-paying alternative school located in a scenic part of the south of England. The second is an Australian inner city, second-chance school catering to young people who, in the main, have very few economic resources. The third is a girls' school in an outer suburb of a major Australian city; it has a high Indigenous population and caters to young women facing difficult social issues. These three schools, whilst drawing on very different student populations and having very different origins, all provide some pointers for what a democratic school might look like. We are not presenting these schools as 'the ideal' as they are all sites that struggle with the effects of trying to implement democratic processes. Indeed as Beane and Apple indicate, 'the work involved in organizing and keeping alive a democratic school is exhausting and ripe with conflict' (1999, p. 13). However, it is these very struggles that we suggest offer insights into what it means to be democratic. We recognize that like many democratic schools these sites operate outside of the public system, which in itself may appear to contradict some of the principles underpinning democratic education. However, we contend that the practices in these schools have something to offer those working towards more democratic education within the public sector. We concur with Fielding who suggests that 'as we approach new crises of political legitimation, participatory traditions of democracy have much to offer public systems of schooling that are witnessing increasing levels of student disaffection and intellectual dereliction'(2013, p. 124).

Feldspar

The Feldspar school has been in existence since 1987 and was set up by a group of teachers and young people concerned about what they deemed to be oppressive practices in mainstream schools. This fee-paying high school is registered for 81 students aged 11–17. Students study subjects up to England's GCSE level. Those students wanting to take Advanced/A Levels (senior secondary) later move to another school. Feldspar has no uniform and the teachers and students are on first-name terms. Additionally, the school has a vegetarian lunch menu in order to ensure that all students can participate in food preparation without the stress of separate menus. Because of the comparative high cost of meat, serving vegetarian lunches enables the school to keep its commitment to providing food sourced from high-quality, organic, Fair Trade produce. Feldspar is grounded in a philosophy that reflects a commitment to democratic principles. The school website outlines this philosophy:

> We believe that everyone should be treated equally, be happy, and have access to good education. At Feldspar, no-one has more power than anyone else, the teachers and students are equal, and there is no headteacher. We try to get rid of all the petty rules, making room for everyone to be happy and free to express themselves in whatever way they feel. The school is democratic, with everyone having their say and equal vote in the weekly school meeting to which everyone may attend (and most do!).

The school's commitment to student freedom and the democratic tradition that underpins the school meeting has often meant that Feldspar is compared with the more famous Summerhill. However, the staff and students at this school are at pains to highlight what they see as their greater commitment to democratic practice than that at Summerhill. For instance, one of the answers to the 'Frequently Asked Questions' on its website makes the following distinction:

> Summerhill is a boarding school and takes children from both primary and secondary ages, and as a result, their social world, how to live together, their rules and punishments have a more dominant focus. Although both schools see the benefits of students making choices about what to study, Feldspar has an academic tutor system . . . that supports and guides those choices that students make. At Feldspar we stress the value of positive choice and benefits gained from facing challenges . . . Summerhill also has a school Head who has veto over all issues. At Feldspar we have no head teacher, and adults have no veto. Students invariably understand when issues such as health and safety are non-negotiable, but everything from wages, staff and student appointments, food and trips is open to discussion.

At the same time as advocating for young people's right to input into everyday decisions that affect them, there is also a concern for developing the students' commitment to the school community which necessarily entails developing certain communal rules. This is also explained on the school website:

> Not having a tie done up correctly affects no-one; missing your washing up means the rest of the washing-up team has more to do. It is this simple approach that makes the few rules at Feldspar beneficial by allowing communal support to all, instead of restriction to the freedom of choice.

Thus the school fosters a sense of personal responsibility within the context of the right to be heard and recognized as an equal member of the school community.

Victoria Meadows

The Victoria Meadows Flexi School began in 1991 in a city park for homeless young people. Sometime later, it moved into an old school premises and at the time of the research was supported by the local City Council and a Catholic schooling organization. The school officially caters to young people aged between 14 and 19 years. However, in reality the school enrols both younger and older students. There is no uniform and it employs both teachers and social workers (no distinction is made between them – they are all referred to as workers) who are called by their first names; and there is a crèche for those students who have their own children. The school provides opportunities for students to achieve the same senior qualifications obtainable in other schools, although the students indicated that there were some restrictions in respect to the curriculum that could be offered due to the size of the school. There is also an expectation that students only attend if they have a difficulty in attending mainstream schools, although the reasons for this can be broad. When we were gathering data the City Council website, for instance, indicated that:

> There are various reasons why you may be unable to attend a main-stream high school. Some reasons are exclusion from school, school/family difficulties or substance abuse, absence from school for a long time because of illness, pregnancy, moving, or you may have special needs.

At the time of the research, the school did not have its own website, although there is now a Facebook site for the school and its past students and, as it has since been incorporated fully into a Catholic flexible schooling network, it relies on the website of this organization to provide details about its existence, philosophies and procedures. When we were conducting our research, the City Council website provided a rather bland description of the school:

> Victoria Meadows Flexi School provides an alternative form of senior school education, and offers an inclusive and non-discriminating learning community to students and teachers alike. The aim of the Victoria Meadows Flexible Learning Centre is to respond to the needs of dis-advantaged young people who have been marginalized from mainstream education.

It described the school's Mission in the following way:

> The Victoria Meadows Flexible Learning Centre has a practical focus, based in the application of four core principles: Rights, Respect, Responsibility, Relationships. The school also has a clear commitment to social justice and stands in solidarity with disadvantaged people of all social, cultural and religious backgrounds.

A youth art organization currently provides a more colourful portrayal:

> This inclusive learning community provides an alternative form of senior school education. It's flexi, it's funky, it's helping young people become active citizens and fulfil their hopes and dreams, it's . . . Victoria Meadows – the Flexi School Community . . . Flexi School is attended by 60+ young people. They are all different shapes and sizes, and get to go after learning opportunities that suit them, within a safe and supportive environment.

The school has a stated commitment to social justice and demonstrates a democratic philosophy in that there is a regular school meeting and students have the opportunity to make decisions regarding what and when they study. There is a range of expectations that are associated with the school. These relate to keeping the school drug-free; making and keeping to a learning plan (with negotiated changes if necessary); taking up opportunities that present themselves; and being engaged with the school. It centres its organization around what is referred to as the '4 Rs': Rights, Respect, Responsibilities and Relationships.

Fernvale

Under the auspices of a Christian organization, Fernvale Education Centre was founded in 1997 in a house in the inner suburb of a major city in Australia. Initially the programme aimed to provide an education and other services to seven young women in government 'care and protection' along with other young women deemed to be at risk of needing such services. Then, as now, many of the young women were/are Indigenous; many were/are young parents. At the time Fernvale was founded, education was delivered via distance education in conjunction with a part-time teacher along with life skills and personal development activities. As people began to hear about Fernvale Education Centre, enrolments grew to a point where the needs of the young people could not be catered to by this small group of workers and the decision was made to seek approval for Fernvale to become a registered independent school. Because most of the students had not succeeded in traditional school structures, the programme was planned to be flexible and innovative. According to its founding school principal:

> We drew on an eclectic mix of research. Democratic Education Theory and the Community Access School concept were central to our approach. All students at the school are treated with *unconditional positive regard*. The success of this model is based on the development of trusting relationships with these young people who have been let down so often by other significant adults in their lives. Our challenge was to create a democratic school with a warm and friendly atmosphere where young people felt welcome and where their input into curriculum development and school organization was valued.

According to the information on its website, Fernvale Education is 'totally committed to social justice for children'. Every week there is a student/staff meeting called 'the Moot'. It is here that the democratic principles of the school are enacted in the discussion of important issues affecting the school and the decisions that flow from them. Fernvale Education Centre became an approved school in 2000, and because the initial group requested it, an optional school uniform was designed by the students.

As a Community Access School, Fernvale aims to reconnect young women to a school community and also to the wider community. According to their website 'making a contribution to community' is a priority for students. Thus, students are encouraged to participate in forums and conferences that allow them to foreground their opinions to government departments seeking the perspectives of young people. Because Fernvale Education Centre connects its young women to a variety of support systems outside the school it is simultaneously teaching them the value of societal structures from which they have been disconnected. Community is claimed to have also been built through Fernvale's inclusive policy towards past students, parents, carers, family members and especially Indigenous Elders. Such people seem to be welcome visitors with many (e.g. Elders) being able to contribute to the cultural life of the school.

At the beginning of 2002, Fernvale Education Centre moved to a new, purpose-built campus in a nearby suburb. True to its democratic principles, students were involved in all stages of the design and appearance of the buildings. Additionally, in 2003, not far from the main school buildings, a smaller campus with a crèche was built for those young women whose needs included child care and more intensive support to enable them to complete their education. Catering to total enrolments of approximately 100 young women, Fernvale offers a regular suite of subjects from years 8 to 10, with particular emphasis on literacy, numeracy and various life skills. However, in the senior school (years 11 and 12), the school offers a range of vocational subjects. If students wish to undertake academic subjects they may do this via distance education. Life skills, personal development and work experience programmes continue to feature throughout the senior years.

Whilst Feldspar, Victoria Meadows and Fernvale are very different they also have much in common. All three schools articulate a concern for young people's rights with concerns for responsibilities located in the well-being of the school community; they have a stated commitment to social justice; seek to incorporate students' voices into the governance of the school; and they are concerned with 'young people in the present' (as opposed to their future 'adult selves'). One of the striking features of all three schools is the high positive regard in which they are held by the young people to whom they cater. According to their public profiles, all three schools continue to operate according to the principles articulated above; however, as the data presented in this book were generated at a specific time at these sites, we present our analyses in the past tense.

As indicated earlier, in the following section, we use Nancy Fraser's (1997, 2010) social justice framework of 'representation', 'distribution' and 'recognition' as the lens through which to view our case studies and the basis on which to conduct our analyses. As noted in our introduction of this chapter, 'parity of participation' in society is affected by political structures, material circumstances and marginalization of some groups on the basis of 'difference'. If we accept that democratic representation is the foundation for achieving distributive and recognitive justice, then self-identified 'democratic' schools become interesting case studies in the pursuit of socially just schooling. Hence, the sense of students having some control over their destiny both in and out of the classroom was the key criterion for selecting the schools considered in this chapter; only one of these schools self-identifies as 'democratic', however, all three schools have embedded democratic *practices* that support the achievement of social justice in other areas of the lives of the students.

We begin with a discussion of governance structures in all three schools, but with a focus upon Feldspar as providing an example of the practices of representational justice; we then examine Victoria Meadows and Fernvale in terms of the lessons they provide for ensuring distributive and recognitive justice. Here it must be noted that we are not claiming that any of these schools provide one perfect model; rather, our intention is to tease out the implications that their practices may contribute towards theories of achieving more socially just schooling.

Representation: democratic governance

It is our contention that socially schools should listen to and value the contributions that both students and workers can make towards the decisions that impact upon their lives. Thus, governance issues are central to determining the extent to which a school truly engages in representative justice in its practices. In many cases it was the apparent lack of student representation and alleged authoritarian nature of mainstream schooling that had led to the young people from all three schools rejecting their original schools. For instance, at Victoria Meadows, Jennifer's story about why she dropped out of her previous school contained critiques of teachers and the lack of opportunity to defend what she perceived to be unfair accusations:

> I didn't like it . . . The teachers, I just didn't like, yeah . . . and I got into trouble for things that I didn't do. Like a text message that was sent from somebody else's phone and I just got suspended for that and I was like, 'Nah, I don't want to be here any more' so I left.

Stories such as these were common across all of the schools represented in this book. The lack of representation or voice within a former school meant that for many of the students it was much easier for them to leave than to put up with what they perceived to be injustices. What is important to acknowledge here is that this marginalization or silencing occurred as a consequence of being a young person and that within the vast majority of schools, regardless of cultural or socio-economic background, students operate within a regime where the authority of the teacher and of school rules are very difficult to challenge. There were a number of commonalities across most of the schools in our study, and in all of the case study schools in this chapter, that worked to ameliorate some of this marginalization. These shared features included calling the teachers by their first names; the lack of a mandated uniform; and respectful treatment of students by teachers. Students in all three of the schools regarded them as critical to the processes of re-engagement. Interestingly, one of the unique aspects of Victoria Meadows was that the school chose not to use the term 'teacher'. All adults were 'workers' regardless of their primary role in the school. This helped to break down barriers between the different types of work being done with young people, for example, teaching, youth support, social work, legal aid and so on. It also worked to distance many of the students from their earlier negative experiences of schooling. For instance, Molly, like other students, was supportive of the term 'worker', and when asked about the teachers at the school, replied:

> The teachers, well we don't call them teachers we call them workers because it's not so formal; it's more like they're your friend – they're here to help you and they're here to teach you. But they're workers . . . and they're very good in the sense that they have lots of patience and they know how to work well with the students and some of them are actually social workers and stuff and youth workers so they've worked with a lot of young people before so it's good.

Justin from Victoria Meadows also explained the importance of calling the teachers by their first names:

> You know it's not Sir, Madam, it's not Mr and Mrs whatever. I couldn't even tell you what half the teachers' last names were . . . Yeah pretty much, they're all you know, like – George, Angela, Carol and, you know, you don't really know their last names. It makes you feel equal not below, like it's not 'Yes Sir, no Sir, three bags full Sir'.

What was interesting here is that Justin, who had had a very difficult time at his previous school, was fully engaged in learning and that the practices that 'make you feel equal not below' were seen as central to supporting this engagement. For example, he went on to explain to us that:

> Like, in English you can sit down, you know . . . at the moment we are actually focusing on debates and things so it's sort of that way anyway but usually you can sit down and we'll discuss something or we bring up a topic and we'll actually sit down and have a full class discussion about it . . . It's more what *your* opinion is about stuff and they're not going to beat you down on every opinion.

The ways in which Victoria Meadows and Fernvale dealt with conflict were also seen as a positive by students from both schools; that students had a sense that an avenue existed for addressing matters related to any injustices they had experienced. For instance at Victoria Meadows, Julie, in providing a critique of mainstream schools, also provided an account of how conflicts were resolved at the school:

> [Mainstream schools] they're very strict, very strict and, not a lot of people like rules and being told what to do, and there's so many boundaries and, discipline; there's too much discipline at normal schools because here we don't get suspended, we don't get expelled or anything. If something happens, if we get in a conflict or something like that we get asked to leave and come back in a few days and then we have a meeting . . . that's how

we solve conflict and it's very helpful that way so we don't feel like we're pushed out away from everyone.

Teachers at Victoria Meadows and Fernvale told us how young people were sometimes asked to go home as a 'circuit breaker' but that they were always welcomed back. Many of the young people at these two schools faced, for instance, severe difficulties in terms of poverty, had to raise children on their own, had a dependence on drugs and/or were living independently. This meant that workers at the school felt that they had to set some ground rules albeit within particular contexts; for instance at Victoria Meadows, this context was their 'Rights, Respect, Responsibility and Relationships' framework. Both workers and students at the schools emphasized to us that their relationships were based on trust and that when students were asked to take some time out they did return to the school and the issue was addressed as a community.

Whilst the Victoria Meadows and Fernvale schools had a commitment to ensuring that students' voices were heard and that there were opportunities for grievances to be aired, of all of the schools in our study it was Feldspar that was the most focused on ensuring that students were integrated fully into the decision-making processes of the school. As with students in the other schools, many of the Feldspar students were critical of the undemocratic student–teacher relationship they had experienced in previous schools. For instance, Holly from Feldspar told us:

> I felt at my old school all the teachers sort of got into their heads that they controlled us and every single thing which you did and in the end it just kind of makes you hate them whether they're a nice person or not.

Similarly the Feldspar students praised the quality of the relationships that existed between them and the teachers and other workers at the schools. Many of the students suggested that the egalitarian and democratic nature of the school promoted a mutual respect between teachers and students (as well as between students). Paige and Amelia, for instance, in discussing the relationship between the quality of teachers and the structure of the school, suggested that the elements of non-compulsion and democracy in the school facilitated this respect for the teachers:

> Paige: I think the teachers approach some things differently and kind of, instead of just you know like, 'Come in, shut up, that's it' . . . I really have a lot of respect for all our teachers.
>
> Amelia: And there's a lot of respect between everyone.

Both students and teachers at Feldspar stressed that *all* members of the school community were *equally* involved in decisions such as the setting of rules; appointment of staff; admission of prospective students; and in shaping the direction of the school. However, the importance of student voice in decision-making in the school did not mean that there was chaos, that the students made oppressive rules or acted irresponsibly. It also did not mean that students were never asked to take time out. However, when they were, it was as a consequence of action taken at a school meeting involving both students and teachers. For instance, one of the students, Riley, explained to us how the school had a few years earlier started to get a bad reputation in the village and that a lot of this had come about, amongst other things, through students smoking in town:

> For one we've made a rule that if you're found under 16 smoking anywhere, because you're in the school, so like parentless, then you get a day's immediate suspension . . . But also, anyone who is smoking, if they're over 16 they have to go somewhere out of sight so they don't upset the local community. And also we don't, we said that kids aren't allowed to run around the streets shouting and playing tag in the streets and stuff because we did have a lot of bad press and it was affecting people coming to the school.

Within Feldspar, Fernvale and Victoria Meadows variously scheduled meetings were used as the main avenue for addressing both the everyday issues of the school as well as sensitive and difficult issues within the school community. In the literature on democratic governance, the role of the school meeting is one area that has attracted significant attention. For instance it is regularly highlighted as the key feature of Summerhill (Neill 1970). It was also a central feature of the schools considered here. All three held regular meetings where various issues facing the students and the school were raised. What differed was the relative power of the students in each school, and in this area, the votes of Feldspar students carried *equal* weight with the teachers. Clearly, within some schools that consider themselves 'democratic' there are limits to the power wielded by students within their regular meetings.

The notion of the 'school meeting' has a long history and, as Fielding (2013) notes, has been present in the government sector of schooling as well as in more radical democratic schools. Fielding's description of the Epping House School in the 1960s suggests that many of the young people that it supported would have been facing similar issues to those faced by the young people attending Victoria Meadows. Epping House was a school at which the students were encouraged 'to understand that the adults were on their side' (2013, p. 126). One way in which this occurred was through the daily school meeting. Fielding indicates that these meetings were underpinned by a commitment to justice. Similar comments could have been made about the meetings at both Victoria Meadows and Feldspar. Whilst the morning meeting, along with other meetings, was clearly an important aspect of the school organization at Victoria Meadows, at Feldspar it was the central feature of the school. One Feldspar teacher, Ava, told us:

> The whole school is built around the idea that the school meeting is at the very heart of the community and that that is the be all and end all, that's

our headteacher, that's our executive, that's what makes the decision and from that comes out the idea that students have personal choice over their education and a say in what subjects they want to do, what lessons they want to do, what interest they want to develop and be taught. And that's a big thing in democratic education, you will see that in democratic schools around the world that call themselves democratic.

The students at the school were also very articulate and passionate about the importance of the school meeting, often stressing to us that the meeting was the place where *all* major decisions affecting the school were made. Riley, a 15-year-old, for example, commented that:

Basically the school meeting has the final definitive say on anything in the school that goes on: expulsions, monetary matters, *anything* at all can be bought up in the school meeting and overruled by everyone; the student body, the teacher body, all together . . . one vote, *exactly* the same, there's not a veto by a head teacher or anything, no, because at Summerhill they have a veto which we don't have.

The meeting was also seen as having educative value. One of the teachers, who had a daughter at the school, explained to us how the school, and in particular the school meeting, had had a dramatic impact upon her daughter:

Rita: The younger one Chelsea, who I was telling you about a moment ago, feels that it's completely changed her life and she's able to do all sorts of things that wouldn't have occurred to her, you know if she'd stayed in the sort of cliquey mainstream, follow the herd-type education. And the fact that we have the school meetings where children talk a lot, and Chelsea was particularly political and articulate – she managed to hone a lot of her skills with the school meeting and generally that gives children huge amounts of confidence.

The school's commitment to democratic governance was also seen by some teachers to have had positive curriculum and pedagogical implications. One teacher, Ian, told us in relation to those subjects that were not part of the compulsory curriculum how involving students in the curriculum decisions had made him more 'creative':

I'm trying to sort of devolve my role as a teacher . . . I make them make all the decisions about what their work is going to be on, what a piece of work is; they do a project so they pick a theme for their project then they have to decide what a piece of work is and all I will do is give them as many options as I can think of and keep the options as broad as possible. Sometimes they don't need any options at all and often I'll go, 'Here's your list to pick from or you can do whatever you want' and often they'll go, 'Well actually I'm going to do this' . . . And then at the end they assess it; so I've written out a set of assessment criteria which I'll go through with them, which I'll show them but it's all based on their enjoyment of the work and the pride they have in the finished product and their assessment of whether they think they've used their time well. So I'm trying to take the teacher out of it so that I become a facilitator.

However, whilst students clearly had an impact upon the curriculum and the meeting, as one teacher had told us, was in effect the school's 'headteacher' and 'executive', teachers did have some autonomy. For instance, Rita told us about the ways in which curriculum decisions were often made at the school, and in her classrooms:

Rita: I mean technically I suppose everything should go to the meeting but, you see a lot of things are delegated so a lot of curriculum things are delegated to the staff . . . you couldn't take everything to the meeting – you wouldn't have time really. Sometimes I say to them, 'I think we'll do such and such a Shakespeare' and sometimes I let them choose but I do sometimes say, 'No we're not going to do that because you're really only choosing a title, you actually don't know any of these plays and I do and, you should probably trust me on this' and they usually go, 'Yeah okay' (laughs).

However, she noted that the support that students gave her was based on trust and that if that trust was breached then they 'would have no hesitation bringing it to the meeting'. For democratic governance to work, such trusting and respectful relationships among students, teachers and workers are necessary.

The governance structures at the three schools represented in this chapter demonstrate a commitment to ensuring that the young people attending them did not feel marginalized or alienated by events and decisions over which they had no control. There was a strong culture within the schools of recognizing that young people when given responsibility will embrace these responsibilities in ways that promote the well-being of the community. Thus there are two sets of lessons emanating for mainstream schools here. The first relates to students' engagement in learning. For example, at Victoria Meadows and Fernvale, many students had not responded well to the disciplinary regimes of their previous schools. Many had been suspended or excluded for a variety of reasons. They looked back at their times in those schools with anger, resentment and/or sadness. Yet of their current school, they spoke of the respect they had for the workers and for the school and what it was trying to do for them. Much of this respect came from the ways in which they were given opportunities to make contributions to the community and to the ways in which they were listened to by the workers. Whilst recognizing the differences between the workers and the students, the relationships that emanated from this respect were seen as being egalitarian. The histories of students at Feldspar were not as troubled as many of those who attended Victoria Meadows and Fernvale. However, students at Feldspar were still highly critical of the ways in which they had felt oppressed by the perceived authoritarian nature of their former schools. These students, too, praised their current school, foregrounding the respectful relationships that grew out of the schools' democratic processes. Such relationships need not be restricted to schools such as Victoria Meadows, Fernvale and Feldspar. What appears to be central here is not the students' dress or appearance, the titles of teachers, or even students' ability to meet deadlines, but their willingness to engage in a community of learners in partnership with teachers. Working on developing such partnerships might well improve mainstream schools' capacities for meeting the educational needs of all students, but especially those for whom schools have traditionally failed.

The second set of lessons relates to the ways in which the school meeting at Feldspar operated as the central decision-making mechanism within the school. The functioning of this meeting was premised on the trust of the students. At this school students knew they could not only air grievances and contribute to matters that affected them, but they could also be held accountable by their peers should they transgress what was deemed to be acceptable behaviour. Students were also trusted to determine what constituted 'acceptable behaviour'. In many mainstream schools the underpinning value is one of *dis*trust of students, often epitomized in various behaviour-management strategies, school rules and classroom expectations; and many behaviours deemed acceptable or unacceptable often having little relevance to the learning process or of creating a harmonious learning community. For example, consider dress rules relating to colour of hair ribbons and socks; and behaviours linked to personal learning styles such as listening to music devices whilst engaging in research activities. Within Feldspar the students learnt how to negotiate complex relationships, how to be responsible for their own actions and those of others, and how to be an active citizen within their community. This environment was not a utopia, and as others have demonstrated is not something that can *only* occur in privileged environments (see for example, Fielding 2013); indeed, Victoria Meadows also used student meetings to make many key decisions. Our data would seem to support the contention that 'the school meeting', configured in a variety of ways to cater to much larger schools, could underpin school organizational processes in many locations.

Distribution: more than just lessons

One might expect that within schools grounded in democratic governance structures, the achievement of distributive and recognitive justice must surely become easier; however, this may be difficult if the established 'democracy' is compromised by admission procedures that limit enrolments to particular groups. For instance, Feldspar charged fees and prospective students and staff had trial days during which they were monitored by existing students and staff to determine whether they would 'fit into the school'. There were barriers in relation to income (potential students) and certain attitudes (both potential students and staff), both of which are keenly related to the circumstances of prospective students. Thus it seems unlikely that some of the young people accepted by Fernvale and Victoria Meadows would have been able to attend Feldspar. In order to protect the Feldspar 'experiment' (as it was described by one of the teachers), admission to its ranks was therefore restricted. In contrast, Fernvale and Victoria Meadows worked with young people from very troubled backgrounds and offered significant support to students in terms of responding to the material conditions that had prevented the students from attending their former schools.

In terms of the ways in which schools like Victoria Meadows and Fernvale demonstrate a concern with distributive forms of social justice, we will focus here on Victoria Meadows. Unlike Feldspar, Victoria Meadows had students who largely came from low socio-economic backgrounds. Whilst there were students in all of our sites who had experienced a variety of problems in their mainstream schools, the differing socio-economic and family backgrounds between those students at flexi schools like Victoria Meadows and the ones attending Feldspar meant that the transition between schools was often, although not always, much easier for those attending Feldspar. Furthermore, the vast majority of students at Victoria Meadows would not have been able to afford the type of fees expected at Feldspar. In this section of the chapter we explore some of the ways in which Victoria Meadows supported those students for whom the ability to attend school was affected by issues of distributive justice.

The students at Victoria Meadows often faced far more difficult out-of-school lives than the students at Feldspar; their personal circumstances sometimes translated into a difficult relationship with their previous schools. For instance, 18-year-old Julie, who was mentioned in Chapter 3, had been to eleven primary schools, three in her last year of primary, and two high schools before falling pregnant at age 14, and she now had two children. She described how she had come to Victoria Meadows four years earlier:

> The principal (at her former school) just basically told me halfway during the year, leave or I'm just going to fail you and expel you at the end of the year. And yeah, I just left. I didn't want to drop out, I didn't want to just do nothing, I wanted to continue and so I looked around in the Yellow Pages (phone book). I looked everywhere then I called my YPP – Young Parents Programme – and they gave me Victoria Meadows's number. And I rung them and they said, 'Yep, yep that's fine come in for an interview.'

Justin, a 19-year-old, explained how he had come to leave his previous school and detailed some of the barriers to an education that he had faced. Both of his parents had died and he had tried living independently and going to a regular high school. He had tried to maintain work whilst studying but had found that that extra commitment brought him into regular conflict with the school authorities leading to his expulsion from the school. In describing the school he had started in year 11:

> [I] struggled and fought with the school the whole time I was there. They made it really difficult for me to study. They didn't want to understand my circumstances. They didn't care. So pretty much I got expelled there. Like before I got expelled I was sitting on an OP [overall position] of one,[1] they didn't give a shit about my grades and pretty much, 'you're a bad person' but even though I was doing really, really good at school they didn't care . . . I pushed my hardest at school, like I still did all my assignments, got them all handed in. I never got anything under an 'A' at school and they didn't care about that, they just more cared about my effort of being at school –'cause I wasn't making up the semester days . . . in the end I just couldn't win the battle. And so I had to leave there and then after that I started working in factories and pretty much almost killing myself with work. For years on end I was just cleaning and did a multitude of jobs. But like the end of last year I was sitting there thinking like I really need to finish my year 11 and 12 and I really wanted to get it done so I could maybe possibly one time in my life have a shot at going to uni.

Many of the schools in our research saw themselves as offering something other than just academic work. In particular, they sought to ensure that material disadvantage did not prevent young people from acquiring an education. This was particularly the case with Victoria Meadows. For example, in order to address the lack of resources and poverty that faced many of the students such as Justin, the school had set in place a range of services to ensure that the students could attend the school. For instance, there was a crèche so that young parents, primarily young women, would be able to access childcare whilst they were studying. There was also, amongst other things, food provided throughout the day, showers, access to social workers who could locate shelters for those needing accommodation and access to legal services for those requiring them. Victoria Meadows thus had a number of redistributive processes in place to ensure that students were able to attend the school and that their financial circumstances did not inhibit their ability to attend school. For instance, students told us how the school reimbursed their train or bus fares when they attended, as one student commented, 'You give them your ticket in the morning and they give you the money back in the afternoon.' Julie, who had two children, also spoke of the support she received from the workers:

> Because I've been on my own since I was 15, I've had to live by myself and had to move a lot so they've been really supportive trying to find somewhere to live. Angela, she's really good – she gives me lots of support.

The intention of the school to address the effects of poverty on students' opportunity to access an education was evident in many interviews. For instance,

Samantha told us in great detail how the workers from the school played a major role in supporting her through some difficult times:

> At the end of last year I moved into a place just nearby with two friends and it was going really well but I had a lot of health issues living on a main road – it was really kind of tough. I had skin irritations, stuff normally you can get just from being so low, and paying higher rent and not having enough for food so the Flexi School really did help me. On a long weekend they've given me stuff out of their fridge to take home to eat and be really understanding if I had to go to the doctor's one day . . . And it's really . . . a huge safety net and a couple of friends here have really helped me to make sure that I don't lose my goal – that I don't lose my drive to keep studying or working.

Sometimes there was also financial help. Tim, for example, told us how he had completely run out of money:

> A couple of weeks back I didn't have any money for transport and I didn't have any money for my medication and I said that and they actually gave us, me and Kylie [girlfriend at the school], twenty dollars so we've got transport and money for my medication so we were alright then.

This support was also noted by Justin, who said:

> Yeah if we had accommodation problems and things . . . Like people like Maria would step up and help out and Monica and that would come in and they'd be like, 'Oh well' because they're more, they're not teachers they're more so like they're like youth consultants and things and with the school it's actively right into the Red Cross.

Another student, Crystal, who had a young son, was grateful for the support she was provided with from the school. She talked of the struggle she had experienced in terms of getting both herself and her baby ready in the morning for school and making the bus on time. However, the facilities at the school made it worth it for her. She noted that: 'The main thing for me is they have a child minder and he doesn't have to go away from me.' Having food at the school was also highly significant. For instance, Crystal also told us: 'We can come and make coffee and toast. It's so much easier when I'm running late and I don't have time to feed my son then I can come here and have breakfast.' The way she was received at school was also important, especially in relation to being able to bring her son to school:

> It's so much different to a school like you have a really good relationship and bond with the teachers and other students. No one looks at you differently, everyone gets along with everyone. Yeah it's just so much better

than a normal school. I hated normal school. I've been in this, like in flexible learning schools since grade 10 but I didn't attend grade 9 very much at [former high school] because I didn't like it.

She also told the story of how a teacher at Victoria Meadows had been supportive when she was close to giving birth:

When he found out that I was pregnant, he got onto some of his friends and he got me a cot, a rocking chair, a pram, sheets, baby clothes. He just gave me the *best* head start that I could have ever possibly gotten.

As such stories indicate, many of the young people from Victoria Meadows faced very challenging life issues, for example, the death of parents, teenage parenthood, homelessness and poverty. Indeed, it was these circumstances that had often facilitated a conflict with the expectations present in their former schools. In some cases this conflict had led to the young person being out of education for many years, and in others, only temporarily. However, what was very apparent in their comments was that the vast majority of these students would not have been in *any* form of education if it were not for the existence of schools such as Victoria Meadows. This school provided a supportive environment that took into account the need to ensure that students could afford to attend; would require support to find accommodation; would on occasions even need to be provided with food, various forms of government assistance, and help to access that assistance. As with the ways in which the schools in this chapter provide lessons for mainstream systems of schooling about issues of representational justice, there are also lessons here about how to take issues of distributive justice into account.

Mainstream education has, as its priority, the academic outcomes of students. That this should be a focus of a school is of course important, although in the current moment this focus often has 'perverse' or anti-educational effects (Lingard and Sellar 2013) that encourages a narrowing of the curriculum and an obsession only with outcomes that are quantifiable. However, for many young people in countries like Australia and England the ability to attend a school is often hampered by factors beyond the school. Education systems frequently seem blind to, or unable to respond to, life circumstances shaped by the debilitating and accumulative effects of poverty that impact upon a young person's ability to comply with schooling expectations. Instead, such effects become central to the construction of students as problems due to, for instance: students' lateness, absence, lack of uniform and failure to pay for excursions or textbook-hire schemes. As demonstrated by schools like Victoria Meadows, clearly, a *re*-distributive form of social justice is necessary to facilitate the educational journeys of our most marginalized young people. We now turn to the third element of Fraser's framework, 'recognition' of, and a valuing of difference. We found this principle at all three schools considered in this chapter but again have chosen to highlight its practice at the site at which it was most explicit: Fernvale Education Centre.

Recognition: acceptance and valuing of difference

Students from all of the schools in this book spoke of the difficulties they had faced in previous schools because they were 'different' and how this had often led to bullying. In many cases the bullying had caused the young people to leave their school. However, it was perhaps Fernvale that best addressed issues of difference. Its students, like those at Victoria Meadows, were largely drawn from low socio-economic populations and like all the flexi schools in this study, it provided much more than just academic lessons. There were youth workers and counsellors at the school; there was assistance with accessing government support agencies; and help in finding accommodation and access to regular meals. However, this was a girls' school that also had a focus on supporting pregnant girls and young mothers along with a strong concern with supporting Indigenous girls. The school was not designed as, nor advertised as, a school just for pregnant girls or young mothers and/or as an Indigenous school. However, it was in these areas that 'difference' was highly valued and, as such, exemplified its commitment to justice issues focused on 'recognition'.

Fernvale Education Centre attracted large numbers of young girls and women who had experienced severe disadvantages. We heard many stories of abuse, domestic violence and poverty. As a consequence, the school directed many of its resources towards providing avenues for students to escape from difficult domestic arrangements. As Sienna in year 12 told us:

> There's youth workers that will help you with Centrelink [government support agency]. They've got Erica up there – she's the counsellor if you have a problem with your parents or your partner or you need a home or something, she'll help you do that. She just helped me leave a domestic violence relationship so she helps with that sort of stuff as well. She's got so many contacts for people who need counselling or legal aid or accommodation. They do awesome things. They offer transport for people who can't get here.

Another girl, Amy, told us:

> Well I have a major depressive disorder and I went to a psych ward for a while and couldn't really deal with the mainstream schooling so searched around looking for a smaller school that had small class sizes.

One of the teachers who was relatively new to the school had been amazed and impressed by the support that was provided to the students. When asked about the strengths of the school she told us:

> The stuff that they help them with here – where are they gonna sleep tonight? Have they got childcare for the kids? They help them with medical needs, they'll take them to the doctor, that type of stuff. See I've never been in schools where they help them with that.

As indicated earlier, the school had originally been set up in a house to address the educational needs of a small group of girls, but as time went on, and the workers in the house were very successful in helping the girls to complete schooling, funding was finally obtained to set up a full time school. Underpinning the construction of this school was a commitment to social justice that was concerned with gender and with Indigenous issues. This commitment played itself out in the construction of facilities, the curriculum and the staffing policies of the school.

Amongst the school facilities was an off-site crèche that was a short walk from the school. Those young women who had children were able to leave them at the crèche with the ability to go back during lunch and recess to ensure that their children were okay. The concentration of these young mothers in one place also facilitated opportunities to create support groups and to access medical services. In recognizing the needs of young mothers the school also acknowledged the importance of flexibility. When one student told us that the school was 'awesome' we asked her to explain why she used that word. Sienna replied:

> They've got a crèche and because my two younger children have high medical needs the school understands that my son goes to physio and has eye appointments and everything like that and they allow me the time off school to go to their appointments.

The flexibility and lack of rules seeking conformity were also contrasted with the young people's previous schools and were given as reasons why Fernvale made it easier for them to attend school. Megan, who had dyed pink hair and eyebrow piercings, told us:

> If you were five seconds late to a class you had to go and sit in the RTC [Responsible Thinking Classroom] whereas at Fernvale it's okay – even if you come into a lesson halfway through because you've been doing something with the counsellor or you had to talk to the principal or something – it'll just be like, 'Okay, that's okay, we're doing this, let's catch up on that and it doesn't matter what you look like as long as you do your work.'

Many of the young mothers and pregnant students spoke of the ways they had been treated in their original schools since falling pregnant. For instance, Megan explained: 'I was pregnant and wasn't allowed to return to Beechtree College because . . . I was going into grade 12 and they said that I'd start a fad for the younger children to all come to school pregnant!' Whilst recognizing that in many cases students faced very difficult life pathways as a result of becoming such young mothers, there was also recognition that students should not have to feel ashamed of being pregnant, as Megan indicated when describing how her pregnancy was differently received at Fernvale in relation to her former school: 'I was pregnant and everyone here was going, "Oh look you're pregnant, look at that little bump" whereas at Beechtree it was like, "Hide it", you know,

"We don't want to see it".' The young women who were pregnant when they arrived at the school had often not had much assistance to prepare for motherhood so Fernvale provided material support for getting ready for the birth of the child. As Megan went on to tell us:

> They actually gave me a list of everything I'm gonna need to buy before the baby comes and it was just like, 'Whoa this is a massive list' but I got it all. Like they even helped some of the girls actually get baby stuff, like, because some people can't afford it so they actually help them and it's good.

The recognition of the difficulties facing many of these young women also led to the school setting up facilities that could be accessed during the school holidays. One young mother, Katrina, told us:

> They put a holiday programme on for us and no other school does that and I find that really good because I'm a mother and I like to enjoy myself and have a bit of a break sometimes and that's what it does. So on holidays I can bring the kids here and then go out.

However, the fact that the school had many mothers and pregnant girls did not mean these students were not fully part of the community or were treated as a separate group. Sienna described the ways in which the different groups at the school interacted: 'I think it's like basically a normal everyday school but you've got mums mixing with the young ones as well.'

In addition to girls who had or were soon to have child-raising responsibilities, there was also a high Indigenous student population. Attracting Indigenous students had not been a stated intention of the school in the original days, but because of the support given to Indigenous girls, the relationship that the school had set up with the local Indigenous community and the embedding of Indigenous perspectives into the curriculum and everyday life of the school, the Indigenous student population had grown to about 60 per cent of the student population. The school deputy principal, Margaret, explained to us how this had occurred:

> When I first came here that wasn't the case . . . It's grown because of our culture of respecting Indigenous culture . . . it has been my agenda to embed real cultural stuff and, can I say that while we all celebrate our cultural days and we all go home and we all feel good about that – to us that's just a celebration of what we're doing . . . we *bring the community* into the classroom and so we've got some pedagogy happening here where 'aunties' [female Aboriginal elders] are telling their stories and girls are telling their stories and out of that we're getting learning outcomes . . . the dancing, and the real cultural stuff is part of our curriculum and our girls go to the local primary schools to demonstrate ochre [earthy pigments used for painting] and dancing – getting our outcomes for their curriculum has encouraged a lot of girls to come here.

The deputy also indicated that one of the consequences of foregrounding Indigenous cultural knowledges was that this had worked to attract students from the Indigenous community school. She expressed some concerns about this. However, she noted that at times students from Fernvale also went the other way to the Indigenous school and that this type of movement gave the students more options than had once existed in this local area. The growth of a larger Indigenous presence also led to the appointment of a teacher with an Indigenous background. One of the key teachers at the school, Kathy, who taught social science was Indigenous and at the time of interview had just moved from the Indigenous community school. She viewed her indigeneity and cultural background as having been key to engaging the Indigenous girls in the curriculum:

I really believe that a lot of the teachings of my old people, the elderly that I grew up with and worked with, the lessons, the knowledge, the information, the respect that they taught me, have helped me to establish myself here and I think that even though the girls may come from homes, how can I explain this, even though we think that the girls don't understand about some of those things, I think that deep down inside there, there's 99 per cent of them understand the key concept of *respect* . . . and I think that we're able to tap into it. We have, the girls go to the elder's sewing circle on Wednesdays. They've got that connection there and this year's theme for NAIDOC[2] is honouring our elders, 'honouring our elders – nurturing our youth'. So we're really tapping into that whole philosophy here at the school.

It was not just her knowledge of Indigenous issues and ways of life that were perceived to be important, but also her experiences. She made a point of drawing upon her own background and that of earlier generations to motivate the students and to make them see the importance of education for Indigenous people:

I say to the girls, you know, 'It's amazing that if I had been born a little bit earlier I may not have even been here at this school, you know just because of the colour of my skin and because of people's rights to education. We have a right to this and so if we can be here and we've got a right then let's do it properly – let's give it our best.'

Many Australian Indigenous people experience racism on a daily basis. Kathy was no exception, but she was able to draw on her experiences of racism and that of others to work with the girls to politicize their own experiences of racism. For example, she told us:

I got told to get out of the classroom because they wanted to talk about Aboriginal people drinking on The Esplanade in Cairns and I can remember my teacher telling me to get out. So I got out thinking, 'Oh this is good I get out of class', but then when I came back and my class mates were telling me, I was the only Black one in my class, and telling me the sorts of things that they were talking about in class you know the racist comments – I probably wasn't in a position to be able to say anything at that stage.

Having Kathy at the school, along with local Indigenous community members, was recognized by many of the teachers as being important for the Indigenous girls at the school. This was seen as a way of highlighting and in a meaningful way incorporating Indigenous perspectives and concerns in to the fabric of the school. This was emphasized by the business and hospitality teacher, Pam, who told us:

> As I said I've only taught a few Indigenous kids in other schools over the years, but I don't think their culture was certainly encouraged to the same extent. You know, you have multicultural days and things like that, but that's just sort of a, you know everybody does it and 'Where are you from and what's your background?' Where here I think things like the elders involved in the school is another great strength. I think having community people involved works a lot better too – that seems to be much more successful and they [students] look up to elders.

However, the school deputy also explained how the increase in large numbers of Indigenous students raised a number of issues for teachers in the school. For instance, she explained how she often organized professional development programmes for the teachers to learn about Indigenous ways of knowing and of learning. She explained that this did not always go well. She gave an example of how she had arranged one session about Indigenous pedagogies that she believed would work with both Indigenous and non-Indigenous students alike. She told us how, in this in-service session there had been a focus on the Indigenous practice of 'yarning'[3] as a means of engaging students at the start of the lesson. She described a conversation she had had with a teacher after this session:

> Like yarning about things first, to set the thing before you introduce content and . . . she came back from her science lesson where she'd taken away this thing and we were giving feedback. She said, 'Well I tried it.' And I said, 'And what did they chat about?' and she said, 'Well I asked them about anything they'd done.' And I said, 'Sorry?' . . . You know I've just spent the last ten years telling teachers, 'Look I will not have the lesson spent where you're all gossiping and talking about nothing.' So I said, 'Well why would you do that?' and she said 'Well you said, "Let's get into this yarning and get our relationship going".' And I said, (I won't mention names) I said, 'Mary Poppins, I meant to learn about the subject you're about to introduce, you know, "Has anyone got a garden?" Like she's doing science, "Anyone got a garden, anybody know anyone who's got one, have you got a garden?"'

However, she went on to say that the administration at the school had learnt to be tolerant of teachers and that the majority of the teachers wanted what was best for the students; just sometimes they did not know how best to achieve this. For this deputy, it was critical that these students did not get a watered-down education. Thus, whilst there were opportunities for obtaining a variety of vocational education certificates, the school administration stressed the need for intellectual inquiry to be in the classrooms and encouraged students to consider university pathways.

At Fernvale, unlike the Indigenous community school, there were both Indigenous and non-Indigenous students. As such, the extent to which the school had a focus on Indigenous issues is quite unusual. The teachers and administration at the school, though, thought that it was important for *all* students to be exposed to the history of Indigenous/non-Indigenous relations in Australia. Kathy often took responsibility for ensuring that this happened. She told us that:

> Look because I'm so passionate about Aboriginal-Islander education, when I do the history lessons I don't talk from a textbook, I talk from life experiences and when we talk about various policies I can show them documents that my great grandfather and my grandfather had to sign. And I think, you know, a touch of that reality – they get shocked. I think they get emotional but then a lot of the girls can connect as well. They can say well, 'Oh yeah that happened to my dad or my nana or my uncle or aunty or grandmother' or whoever.

When asked if she thought that it was beneficial for the non-Indigenous girls to be exposed to Indigenous cultural knowledges, the deputy replied: 'Definitely, definitely, they don't have to come here, if they don't like it they don't have to come here.' This did not mean that there were never any issues or tensions related to race. As Kathy indicated, 'I think there are tensions within the school occasionally as issues and concerns ebb and flow in the community but I think on the whole we're very positive towards everybody. It's a really inclusive place to be.' This was supported by comments made by the deputy who indicated that these tensions often worked themselves out, although the school often worked hard to ensure that such tensions were resolved. She explained to us that one year they had had a very racist cohort of year 11 students. She told us how many of the girls would make assumptions about Indigenous culture based on premises such as that they had an Indigenous 'person living in our street'. She argued that this racism was fuelled by the school having particular programmes for the Indigenous girls, which included taking the whole year 12 Indigenous group to an overnight Indigenous music festival. Her feeling was that this racism was the product of the Indigenous and non-Indigenous students not knowing each other well. As such the school worked hard on providing opportunities for the students to come together in various activities.

In many schools that cater to populations of students similar to those being supported by Fernvale, there is often an overwhelming sense of despair, of frustration, of lack of connection to the school and a lack of positive experiences on the part of both students and teachers (Smyth and Hattam 2004; White and Wyn 2008; Dillabough and Kennelly 2010). Despite the occasional tensions at the school and the difficulties that were faced by many of the girls and young women, the opposite was the case here. Teachers seemed to have an understanding that when students were having a bad day it was not personal in relation to them. For example, Pam, a business hospitality teacher, who had taught in a variety of Catholic schools and had been at this school for three years said:

> When things go wrong often I've learnt that it's got nothing to do with me; it's something that's happening outside of school. They often either go with a youth worker to see our counsellor or they leave the room for a period of time, let steam off and then they'll come back. And I've found it very interesting because I've had girls that completely lose it and ten minutes later they'll be back and everything's fine again.

When asked how she liked working at the school Kathy told us:

> I'm loving it, absolutely loving it. It has a spirit of freedom and also – the inclusive approach that the school takes and the positive regards stuff, it is good. We do hear girls swearing and we have a few girls throw a few tantrums every now and again, but so would I if I was in her situation, so would I.

The students also had a sense of the teachers not being disapproving or disparaging of their life circumstances or the various situations that had brought them to their current state. For the students we spoke to, the focus of the school appeared to be on the present and on helping them to complete school and to overcome any barriers that might be preventing this from happening. Amy for instance, the student who had told us that she had at one time been confined to a psychiatric ward, explained that:

> They don't judge you by what is happening in your home life. They'll support you all the way but they won't tell you, 'Absolutely not, you can't come here any more.' They say, 'If . . . you're having a hard time you can just come in.' It feels more like they're trying to help you than any other school.

Many of the teachers had spoken to us about how respectful the girls were, even on their bad days. The students also spoke of the respect that *they* received at the school from teachers. For many of them it was the defining aspect of the school. For instance, Megan told us:

> Like, it allows us to be adults and make our own decisions. If we don't want to work then they'll say, 'Okay well, at the end of the day it's your decision if you don't want to work; it's not going to be good for you but we're not going to force you.'

Amy noted quite powerfully that one of the major strengths of the school was that, 'They treat us like the people that we could be without that support kind of thing.' When asked what the underpinning philosophy of the school was, one of the teachers, Brenda, indicated that, 'It's based on unconditional love or positive regard and I guess second chances.'

That the school made a difference in students' lives was captured as well in comments made by Sienna, who told us that it took her two-and-a-half hours to get to the school. She had left school when she was 14, when she first fell pregnant; she was now approaching 20 and had three sons. She found out about the school from the daughter of a woman to whom she regularly sold drugs. She became friends with the daughter who was attending the school. This girl told her that she would be able to go back to education and that having children was not a problem. She informed us: 'If my friend had never told me about it I would still probably be sitting at home.' She also told us how now she had given up drugs, was focusing on being a mother and looking for a way to get into university.

Fernvale's focus on supporting and valuing pregnant young women, young mothers and/or Indigenous young women demonstrates the ways in which a school that takes into account the differing needs of its students can retain and engage students who have not previously fared well within the education system. As with Victoria Meadows, having a crèche and support for young mothers and pregnant girls ensured that these young women were able to attend school. What became apparent to us through this research was that despite support structures that are designed to keep such young women in education (see for example, Department of Education, Training and Employment (QLD) 2011; Dawson and Hosie 2005), many girls who become pregnant are encouraged to leave their schools (see also Vincent and Thomson 2010). Two of the schools considered in this chapter demonstrate the positive effects of providing structures that support an ongoing engagement with education despite the challenges of early parenthood.

Fernvale also provided insights into the ways in which schools can integrate Indigenous knowledges into the curriculum, support the retention of Indigenous students in schooling and challenge racist attitudes and values (see also Keddie and Williams 2012; Keddie 2013). This was a school that was not designed to be an Indigenous school. Its primary aim had been to support young women who had been disenfranchised by the education system because of their life circumstances. However, due to a stated commitment to issues of recognitive justice within all areas of the school, Indigenous students have been made to feel welcome and the school has responded even further through a variety of support networks.

Making a difference: parity of participation

In this chapter, we have not meant to imply that each of these schools had only one focus. As Fraser's (2010) work indicates, none of these forms of justice or injustice are primary; ensuring parity of participation requires addressing all of them at the one time. All the schools considered here do this to varying degrees. For instance, whilst we have focused on the democratic organization of Feldspar, both Victoria Meadows and Fernvale were also concerned about issues of student representation. Distributive injustices clearly impact more greatly on the students attending the flexible schools than they do on those students attending schools such as Feldspar. However, whilst Victoria Meadows and Fernvale were schools that catered to highly disadvantaged young people and Feldspar charged fees, it would be a mistake to construct Feldspar as a 'rich school' that cared nothing for distributive issues. Feldspar was not a wealthy independent school and there was a sense that it did at times support those students who were less well off. For example, Joseph, a 17-year-old from Barcelona in his third year at the school, was living independently and required assistance from the school in order to remain there. He did not see himself as being academically skilled, and was unsure about what he would do when he left the school. He told us:

> I don't want to go to college because I'm not very good at studying so I just, I made a little agreement with Ciaron and with another guy who's a builder who works here in the school as well, and if I could stay here for another year and work with him and get some extra money and I'll teach the Spanish and do other stuff for not having to pay to the school.

That the school was fee-paying also did not translate into the school having outstanding facilities. In a number of areas there was a shortage of resources. For example, the science facilities would not have been as good as many of those found in government schools.

Finally, whilst highlighting Fernvale's commitment to valuing difference, both Victoria Meadows and Feldspar clearly addressed issues of difference and recognition. For example, 20-year-old Zac from Victoria Meadows, who left his previous school in the middle of year 12, described how he had left because he had been bullied by both students and teachers: 'I was different.' This occurred, he suggested, because he was, 'from a country town and I was the only person with the alternative lifestyle so I was really outcasted (sic)'; but this had changed at Victoria Meadows. For many of the students at Victoria Meadows 'misrecognition' in their previous school was compounded by economic injustices. However, there were also students at Victoria Meadows who had made a conscious choice to attend the school despite having the resources to attend private schools. For instance, Vanessa had chosen Victoria Meadows because of the way she could 'be herself' at the school. In her searches, she had been to both a private and a government school and had found them not too dissimilar in their climates:

> I was in a mainstream school – Catholic education, for three years from year 8 'til year 10. I was having complications with bullying and stuff like that, just wasn't really finding it easy to do my work and putting my head down so I decided to change to another mainstream school and I decided to go to a state school for two months and I realized that it wasn't the school it was just the whole system. I just couldn't deal with the way that they were

teaching the kids. I wasn't getting enough attention and so I stopped going to school. I was having a bit of trouble for a while, I couldn't find anything and then my friends referred me to here.

Vanessa's comments about 'having complications with bullying and stuff like that' at previous schools were also reflected in student observations at Feldspar School. For instance, Holly told us how, 'I got quite badly bullied at [previous school].' However, at Feldspar there were many young people who (often with their families) had made a conscious decision to select this school as a first choice because of its philosophy. Unlike the vast majority of young people at Victoria Meadows who had tried mainstream schooling and had left with a sense of bitterness, the students at Feldspar had families who had chosen an alternative school. For the Victoria Meadows students, the school represented another (perhaps *last*) chance to complete their schooling.

Within all the schools there were students who could be perceived to be alternative or different because of their appearance. For instance, Molly from Victoria Meadows, who was dressed in gothic black when we interviewed her, told us how difference was not tolerated at her previous school and that for her being different was important to her sense of being a 'free spirit':

> I didn't like the uniforms and stuff (slight laugh) definitely because I'm more of a free spiritual person like, today I'm wearing this, I mean tomorrow I'll be wearing something completely different! Like I'll be wearing, I don't know, colours and stuff like I'm not really into having a set way of looking and being because I don't believe that a school should teach you how to look or how to be; they're just there to teach you how to do maths, English and the subjects you need in order to make it; the rest of it is *your* choice in life.

The critique of uniforms, and the way in which they prevented students from 'expressing themselves', was also evident at Feldspar. Riley, a 15-year-old who was in his third and final year at the school, noted that previously he had been at an 'authoritarian' private school that had a strict uniform policy involving a tie and blazer, something he now found 'unimaginable'. He said of that school:

> As I got older it kind of felt really quite crushing and embarrassingly authoritarian in the very old-fashioned way because I think it was kind of a school where they had high feelings for themselves. They had lots of false illusions of grandeur.

In all three schools students told us how there was very little bullying at their current school. Across the schools words such as 'community', 'family', 'respectful', 'easy-going' and 'non-judgemental' were used by students to describe their schools. For example, 19-year-old Jennifer noted that at Victoria Meadows, 'people don't judge you here either, like there's no bullying or anything like that. Everybody gets along because they all know that we're all in the same situation.' The lack of bullying was attributed to a number of factors that included an acceptance of difference; the small size of the schools; the culture of respect operating between the teachers and students and among students; and the regular school meeting. Additionally, the overarching focus of the schools on democratic governance clearly impacted upon the schools' commitment to recognitive justice. These three schools in their own distinctive ways provided much support to young people who had rejected or been rejected by the mainstream. As such they were concerned that the students who attended the schools experienced socially just practices and thus provide lessons for the broader educational community.

Conclusion

We are not suggesting that any of these three schools are perfect or that they represent the ideal school. However, what we do suggest is that as 'oppositional alternative schools' they push boundaries of thinking in terms of what is *possible*. It is perhaps difficult to imagine a school run by students and teachers through a direct democratic process, especially when this includes decisions about the employment of teachers and determining their salaries. However, Feldspar demonstrates that it can work. There are clearly times when it is difficult for both students and teachers and times when things go awry. That being said, there is ample evidence, as people interviewed for this book have indicated, that the mainstream is also difficult for many young people and teachers. What is different is that when times are tough at Feldspar, students and teachers have a clearly recognized avenue through which their claims for justice can be heard. In the hierarchical structures of mainstream schools, this is often more difficult. Similarly, both Victoria Meadows and Fernvale demonstrate what is possible when a school goes beyond just a concern with the academic outcomes and focuses on the emotional and material needs of young people. What these schools demonstrate is that whilst schools in general, and the teachers within them, have little control over the broader sets of socio-economic injustices impacting upon students, there are actions that can be taken to ensure that acquiring an education is possible. It is perhaps not too difficult to imagine schools as places where young people can access meals, information about housing, legal aid, showers, financial support, crèches and counselling. What is more difficult is imagining many mainstream schools taking up the challenge of creating such a place when many of the students who require this support are not those who meet the criteria of the ideal neo-liberal student subject, and indeed may be seen as damaging to the school's image in the current market place.

However, at a time when there is a supposed concern with improving school completion, it would seem foolish not to be looking at the ways in which schools such as Victoria Meadows and Fernvale have facilitated these highly discriminated-against young people's engagement with learning. Fernvale also opens up visions of what schools that take on the task of challenging injustices based on gender and race might look like. In many education systems there is a high degree of rhetoric about making schools more inclusive for students from marginalized backgrounds. However, as many of the young women in our study indicated, there is very little support across education systems for those who fall pregnant or have a child (or children) whilst at school. Again, both Fernvale and Victoria Meadows indicate the kinds of support that can be introduced in order to ensure that such young women's education does not conclude at a time when their life chances are already likely to have been narrowed by the extra responsibilities that they have taken or are about to take on. Fernvale also demonstrates what it means to be a school that works to address injustices shaped through a very long history of colonial oppression. At a time when there is significant policy rhetoric about 'closing gaps' and addressing the appalling state of Indigenous disadvantage in Australia, with very little actual effect in mainstream schools, Fernvale is demonstrating what a school that is not an Indigenous community school can do to make a difference by supporting young Indigenous people whilst also ensuring that non-Indigenous students' knowledge about and experience with Indigenous communities are broadened. As such, exploring Fernvale's practices can make a significant contribution to understanding what needs to be done for schools to challenge cultural injustices. As we say elsewhere in the book, it is unlikely that these schools can be replicated; circumstances and local conditions have affected what these schools are. However, we think that a consideration of what these schools have achieved through their various approaches to tackling injustices has much to offer a conversation about how to create a more socially just education system. We take this up in the concluding chapter.

Notes

1 An OP is a Queensland final year student's *overall position* in a state-wide rank order based on their academic achievements.
2 NAIDOC – National Aborigines and Islanders Day Observance Committee – Week celebrations are held across Australia each July to celebrate the history, culture and achievements of Aboriginal and Torres Strait Islander peoples.
3 Yarning Circles are spaces where the community can come together as one, where stories are shared and all are welcome.

7 Conclusion

Lessons from the margins

Instead of schools as 'high performance organisations' we need schools as 'person-centred communities' . . . or some other model that places human flourishing at the heart of our chosen educational processes. What we cannot do is continue as we are but more persistently and more intensely . . . we have to break free from our current modes of thinking and exhibit 'a preparedness to think radically outside the frame'.

(Fielding 2001, p. 13)

It is time for a 're-imagining' of what schools could be. Indeed, given the vast amounts of educational research published each year, it is long overdue. Yet, the dominant schooling paradigm of the twenty-first century continues to echo its industrial antecedents and reflect the current neo-liberal ethos of the marketplace. The neo-liberal *raison d'être* is to make a *profit*, to create *new opportunities* for profit and to induce us into self-governance as a 'willing, self-governing entre-preneurial' (Ball 2012, p. 145), and ostensibly 'free' to shape individual pathways to success. Such a paradigm is premised on individual responsibility and thus allows the state to step back from its obligations towards the common good. However, given the wealth of research critiquing the influence of neo-liberalism and its impact upon education and social justice (see for example, Torres 2009; Rizvi and Lingard 2010; Lingard 2011; Ball 2012, 2006; Apple 2013, 2007, 2000) it is not our intention to dwell on it here; we only wish to remind our read-ers of its ubiquitous presence as further noted by Stephen Ball in relation to how neo-liberalism makes us into:

Neoliberal subjects enmeshed in the *powers of freedom* . . . oppress[ed] . . . through anxieties and opportunities, not by constraint but by incitement and measurement and comparison. This happens in mundane ways as we work on ourselves and others.

(2012, p. 145)

In educational terms, 'profits' reside in the creation of particular types of human capital required to ensure the long-term economic prospects of the state.

'Self-governance' resides in the responsibility of individuals to 'invest' their time and abilities and 'compete' for their personal share of the profits. Regimes of accountability, testing and measuring ensure the 'winners' are separated from the 'losers'; it is the 'outcome' that matters – whether that be schools ranking highly in league tables or systems gaining top scores in international examinations such as TIMSS and PISA. Such 'success' is what might be described as the 'high performance' alluded to in the above comment by Michael Fielding. Challenging such a vision of schooling is at the heart of this book. In the preceding chapters we have introduced many examples of a 'flourishing of the human heart' in the schools we visited; and we suggest that it is their example, along with the stories of their workers and students, that provide some clear directions for changing the ways in which we currently understand schooling, inviting us to think radically outside the frame.

The schools and centres described in this book are not presented as ideals, nor have we sought to romanticize them; rather, we have presented them as starting points for meaningful discussions about their practices and philosophies so that we and others may continue to advocate for systems of education that are fairer to all young people. In particular, we would suggest that there are some immediate lessons in their practices for mainstream schools, lessons that could ameliorate some of the issues that currently lead to significant levels of schooling dissatisfaction and school refusal along with rising numbers of official suspensions and expulsions. We contend that there are some key systemic responses to principles arising from our data that may serve to guide those educators dedicated to the project of considering what a more socially just system of schooling might look like (Francis and Mills 2012b). These responses pertain to the following:

- youth support structures that address the socio-economic, emotional, mental and personal needs of young people;
- school cultures that are inclusive, actively recognize and support marginalized cultural groups;
- school governance structures that ensure that all students and workers have a meaningful voice in making justice claims on the organization; and
- providing learning pathways that are valued, challenging and take student differences into account.

Towards socially just schooling structures and environments

Clearly, schools cannot fix the existing inequalities and injustices of a society. However, they can respond to the consequences that flow from them. This of course requires an investment of money and material goods sufficient to the task. Unfortunately, in times of economic uncertainty what are deemed to be 'non-core' services in schools may be the first to go. For example, the number of school guidance officers in Queensland has been recently reduced because, according to the newly elected Education Minister, 'the Labor government legacy meant there was not enough money in the kitty and chaplains would do instead' (Chilcott and McDonald 2012, p. 1). In the UK, the Institute for Fiscal Studies has warned that the 20 per cent spending cuts to youth services and 16–19 education by the Coalition would have severe consequences for many young people (Gilani 2011). Data presented in this book demonstrate the significance of material support. Some of the most basic necessities were provided by the alternative sites we visited: transport, food, accommodation and items of clothing, as illustrated in the following comment from Pauline, the teacher in charge at Woodlands:

> We have a shower here; a lot of the students have poor living conditions
> . . . We feed them, we talk to them. I suppose we care, you know, and
> hopefully we know each and every student and what they want to do.

Within all our flexible learning centre research sites young people had access to workers who were able to assist (either directly or through referrals) with health and welfare issues. Only when these contextual factors were being addressed could our young participants begin to refocus on their learning and move their lives in new directions. In our post-socialist neo-liberal world, claims for such distributive justice have been challenged, first, by what Ball (2012) refers to as a 'culture of advanced individualism' (p. 145); such a culture presents significant risks for people, particularly young people, who may not have the personal and material resources for shaping the 'require[d] performance of an entrepreneurial self' (White and Wyn 2013, p. 13). Second, distributive justice claims have at times been seen to compete with claims for recognition of difference, for example, around claims for greater gender justice. However, as Nancy Fraser has argued, the recasting of social justice claims from distribution to recognition creates a false dichotomy:

> As the center of political gravity seems to shift from redistribution to
> recognition, and egalitarian commitments appear to recede, a globalizing
> wall-to-wall capitalism is increasingly marketing social relations, eroding
> social protections, and worsening the life chances of billions.
>
> (Fraser 1997, p. 3)

This splintering of justice issues merely serves to compound the problems of the marginalized, and thus Fraser's (2010) multidimensional 'justice framework' takes into account not only distribution and recognition but also political justice via notions of representation. From our data it is clear that distributive forms of justice were an 'enabling force' for the young people we interviewed. The following comment from Sienna, a young mother attending Fernvale Education Centre who hoped to become a teacher, summed up the impact of being at a school where she had access to health and welfare support including childcare: 'I wouldn't have bothered coming back if I didn't find this school.' The impacts of poverty and neglect on young people *can* be addressed through common schooling if there is sufficient political will by governments to re-assume responsibility for social malaises and prioritize the funds that are needed for wraparound social services that are easily accessed by young people.

Such support structures ensure that young people who have been denied access to an education due to financially difficult circumstances are able to attend school. However, ensuring that they are retained in school requires a school environment that actively demonstrates to students that they are wanted and valued. Bearing in mind Fraser's justice triad of distribution, recognition and representation, we thus argue that distributive justice, whilst vital in and of itself, is not enough *by itself*, to progress the social and political claims of the marginalized. Rather than attempting to answer to *competing* justice claims in isolation, justice responses need to be holistic in nature.

As noted earlier in this book, traditional structures of schooling, as they mostly exist in the mainstream, are hierarchical and shaped by the dominant culture. Within the Global North, dominant cultures have their roots in Anglo-European heritages that include historical inequities for females, sexual minorities and people of colour. Also entrenched is a largely deficit view of young people that continues to influence the cultures of schools in terms of rules pertaining to dress, responses to authority and authority figures and decision-making processes. We acknowledge that there are issues of care and protection for children, but as these young people move into high school this argument loses cogency. Essentially, there seems to be a lack of trust in young people to act responsibly – maybe even a *fear* that should adult educators relinquish their hold on 'absolute power' over their students, chaos will ensue. In times of economic and social uncertainty, the perceived need to 'control' young people may increase. Moral panics about falling 'standards' support the current neo-liberal educational discourses of standardized testing along with the introduction of greater powers for school principals and managers to 'discipline' unruly students. Young people in schools who do not fit the 'norm' in terms of their learning and behaviour often face either medical or behavioural intervention. Thus, the 'failure' to develop in a predetermined socially acceptable manner is alternately pathologized or punished.

Barry takes up this point when arguing that 'policy tends to blame young people for their own circumstances' (2005, p. 239) and that processes of age-discrimination deny them access to financial and social resources; moreover, they are denied full social inclusion via a political voice and recognition for achievements because their chronological age deems them to be 'less than adult'. Thus, there is a lack of reciprocity in the relations between adults/teachers and young people/students; there is a lack of *mutual* respect. This view is supported by White and Wyn (2013), who argue that the consequences of moral panics about youth, particularly working-class and/or ethnic minority youth contribute to deficit constructions of young people that elicit generalized fears that shape perceptions of, and relations with, this segment of the population. Thus, faced with the need to market their school and respond to the anxieties of the community, principals and managers are unlikely to institute democratic schooling practices, or forms of 'representational justice'. Our data, however, indicate that to do so is not only feasible, it is educationally advantageous.

Within both the flexible learning centres and the democratic schools in this study, we observed school cultures that took into account the need for representational justice: student voice; mutual respect between young people and adults; and equality of social positioning through the use of first names for adults as well as for the young people. There was a continuum of decision-making power vested in the students across the participating centres and schools, but all subscribed to student voice as one of their key principles; and for young people attending the democratic schools, the importance of their 'voice' was something they valued. The following comment by Alicia, a student from Distincta College, about the school meetings exemplifies this sense of responsibility:

> If it's pretty important issues then we usually go over time [with the meeting] and, sometimes I've stayed till like six [o'clock] or something, really! . . . So I think they're very important and they really work problems out.

As well as finding examples of practices and policies that promoted distributive and representational justice, we also observed recognitive justice in action in the centres and schools participating in this research. All sites promoted values of respect for and recognition of 'difference' in all its manifestations so that the young people who attended could relax into journeys of identity-making without the fear of bullying and discrimination, and there were high expectations for all regardless of their social backgrounds. At St Ebenezer we talked to a cross-dressing young man wearing make-up; he loved science and aspired to attend Cambridge University. Although St Ebenezer is a fee-paying independent school, its democratic ethos clearly separates it from many mainstream independent schools who abide by traditional uniforms and school cultures. The freedom to try on different 'selves' was highly valued across all sites regardless of the economic circumstances of the students. We heard tales of suspensions from mainstream schools for brightly coloured hair, piercings and wearing the wrong-coloured shirts. At the alternative sites, workers looked beneath such superficial exteriors and taught young people to do the same for each other. Consequently, the relationships that flourished in these centres and schools were grounded in an ethos of *positive* instruction. Relations were such that young people trusted the workers who explained 'rules' rather than imposed them from an authoritarian position of power. For example Callum, from Woodlands Flexi School, recalled the different approach to things like swearing:

> Like if you swear by accident yeah like they'll just like talk to you about it or something and like at another school, I got like the work done, the teacher went through the book and he said he couldn't find it but I actually did it and I was like, 'that's bullshit' and I got suspended for that.

Shirley, a teacher from Ertonia Flexible Learning Centre, made the rueful observation that the school environment provided something of a safe haven for young people who came from very troubled backgrounds:

> Their home life is completely different to school. A couple of [our] kids go out in the evening after school. They are on the streets with either drugs or guns. Luckily for us, they tend to keep their two lives separate. When at the centre, they do respect the staff, they do respect the centre and they don't bring – they have *never* brought trouble near the centre.

What is frustrating for those who work with young people is that there are so many relational issues with adults that *could* be fixed – quite easily – if such adults were willing to change the ways in which they interact with young people. This is something that requires an attitudinal shift; it could be implemented quite easily in mainstream schools without any material cost, however that is probably wishful thinking. So entrenched is the view that young people need stringent mechanisms of control, particularly whilst at school, that it would probably require a reasonably significant investment of funds dedicated to the education of personnel in order to change school cultures. As recounted earlier in the book, one of the most enduring, and warmest memories from our many visits to alternative education sites was that of Robert, the headteacher of St Ebenezer, having lunch with a young person of about 13. We are convinced that such models of teacher/worker–student relations, like this – and many others – that we observed in our research schools can provide a templates for change in the mainstream.

Learning pathways

In this book we have described a range of alternative schools that may be further divided according to their curriculum offerings. All sites attempted to cater to the specific needs of their students. However, the fee-paying democratic schools offered a more traditional academic curriculum that also allowed young people to follow artistic and/or vocational pathways if they wished. Due to the small size of most of the flexible learning centres, teachers had to be skilled in the construction of individualized pathways as best they could, sometimes utilizing the support of distance education. However, some provided their students with pathways to universities, further education and training as well as employment. All provided young people with the possibility of acquiring a qualification that represented an opportunity to demonstrate academic success. The latter represented one of the main criteria for selection in this research.

For this study we avoided behaviour-management centres and programmes that attempted to 'fix' the young people and then send them back to the same environment. For similar reasons we discounted short courses (for example, courses that focused on areas that could be classed as hobbies or personal development) because we believe that whilst such offerings may keep young people busy for a short period of time, they generally do not lead to significant academic or vocational credentials that enable young people to progress their lives towards more substantial goals; and the young people we interviewed certainly had goals that were consistent with the dreams and aspirations of the general schooling populace. Across all sites young people talked of going to university or college (academic and vocational); they wanted to be musicians, hairdressers, health workers; IT workers; veterinarians and mechanics (to name but a few). The main distinction in respect to the achievement of goals of our student participants rested with their personal backgrounds. The majority of those who attended the fee-paying democratic schools took it as given that they would go to university or college; they had more resources (emotional and material) to support them and clearly they had social networks that encouraged their dreams. For many of the young people who attended the flexible learning centres, the chance to dream, to plan and to achieve their goals only eventuated *because* they were attending that centre. Many of *these* young people had been constructed in deficit ways throughout much of their schooling; additionally, many suffered from the debilitating effects of poverty, neglect or illness and had come to view themselves as failures. As we spoke to these young people we were constantly amazed by their resilience and moved by their newly found hope for themselves and their future. For example Molly, who had a troubled past and had dropped out of her mainstream school after significant conflicts with teachers, was now exuberant in her newfound confidence at Victoria Meadows:

> I either want to go and work in a homeless shelter for a while and then go into the Aboriginal areas and do relief work there and then take that around the world because then when I'm in Europe I can do homeless stuff and work or I want to focus on my band and work with that (laughs) or I want to just make money and then travel, and then make more money and then travel (laughs).

There was also Katrina from Fernvale who had left school at 14 and was now 20 and a young mother who wanted to give back something of the support she had received from her school. She told us that her goal was to 'become a housing manager or [work] just somewhere in the community services sector – just work in the community services sector; aged care, youth worker, housing manager – just anything along those lines'. The young people who attended the flexible learning sites were candid in their comments that they would not have been in any form of education or training had it not been for the existence of their centre.

Programmes at the flexible sites were student-centred. They utilized learning plans that began at the point where students were at and built from there. Some young people needed more help with literacy and numeracy whilst others were able to engage directly with the academic and/or vocational offerings. The important thing was that the learning plans were designed around the specific needs and goals of each student. Thus the young people could see the relevance of the curriculum and they were keen to use it as a stepping stone towards the achievement of their goals. Scaffolding of tasks meant that students experienced academic 'success', often for the first time in their lives; such achievements, along with the nurturing environments and personalized teaching styles evident in the alternative sites, encouraged the young people to believe in themselves and hope for their futures. Students such as David, who attended Cave Street Flexi School, once believed that he 'was one of the dumbest people in the class' at his mainstream school. He was 16 and although he could only manage year 9 tasks, after only two months at the alternative site he was making good progress and had grown in confidence, commenting:

> I feel a lot better about myself now with the teachers helping us [and you] just work at your own pace . . . Learnt more here than I did at normal school anyway in the two months that I've been here.

Most of the teachers we interviewed for this research had struggled with the structures of traditionally organized mainstream schooling systems that now also demanded that they operate within the constraints of increasingly prescribed curricula and preparation for standardized tests. Data indicate that such issues were significant factors in their move to the alternative sector. They told us that they wanted to teach in ways that were sensitive to the holistic needs of their students, whom they viewed as being more than a set of 'outcomes' to be measured against some kind of predetermined 'standard'. In respect to pedagogy, teachers across all sites worked in very similar ways. Whilst having high expectations for behaviour of the young people, the teachers were non-judgemental. The young people had a fresh start to start their education. Thus the *relationship* between the teachers and their students was fundamental to re-engagement in learning, as illustrated in this short excerpt from Elaine at West Canal Alternative School:

> We have a 'no label' approach. So usually these pupils come with a file this big. So Hayley looks at that. She will highlight anything of the stuff that's of importance, if we need to put anything in place, like risk assessments, et cetera, for that pupil. But then that file goes in the cupboard, kind of thing. It's always there but it's kind of 'I don't want to know if Jimmy's done this at this school five years ago.' I'm not interested. 'Jimmy's got a clean slate. Let's give him a go,' and things like that. And they quite like that.

Data consistently and constantly affirm the importance to pedagogy of positive and caring relationships between teachers and students. For example, we were told by Jane at Woodlands Flexi School she had had a terrible time at her previous school which included a verbal fight with a teacher because 'I didn't know what a noun was.' She described her current school as 'the best school ever because . . . it's just really laidback and awesome'. She went on to tell us:

> Well they don't just say like, 'Here's the work you have to do it', like they actually explain how to do it and everything on the board first. Yeah and if you need help they'll explain it to you personally . . . Like they don't, they're still teachers but they talk to you more like, not teaching just like, more like a mate kind of.

Clearly mainstream schools offer a variety of learning opportunities to their students. However, they also have large classes and teachers who are often time-poor because of increasing burdens of accountability. This is a situation that is detrimental to both students and their teachers; it facilitates a sense of failure for all involved as young people disengage and resist and teachers struggle to 'control' their students and 'enforce' a curriculum that often lacks relevance to the young people. There is a clear lesson here for mainstream schools.

Final thoughts

We are not suggesting that the various practices that are in evidence at any of the schools considered in this book are easily transferred from one setting to another. Rather, what we have sought to do is to provide, in concert with Slee (2011, p. 152) 'exemplars of irregular schooling as beacons of hope'. We are at the same time concerned with what Thrupp (1999) refers to as the 'social class segregation of schooling' (see also Connell 1994). The two sets of schools that we have considered in this book fall at either ends of the spectrum of such segregation. The young people at St Ebenezer could not be more different socially and economically than those, mostly boys, attending The Garage. Thus, the important focus of this study, as we have suggested throughout this book, is about *learning from* alternative schools. We do not want to suggest that the answer to providing a more socially just education system is to create more of these schools. We suggest that despite the positives emanating from these sites, creating more of either type may not be in the interests of a socially just education system.

Not all students are financially able to secure the benefits of the democratic schools. Whilst these schools often cater to students who, for instance, have been bullied or oppressed because of their difference; have been suspended or expelled from mainstream schools for challenges to authority; or have rejected traditional curricula and pedagogical practices, they are often only accessible to students from middle-class backgrounds. We would argue that creating more options for the middle class is not necessarily in the interest of a socially just education system.

Many students from poorer backgrounds have had similar experiences to those students in the democratic schools who were disillusioned with mainstream schooling. However, they have also had to contend with a range of other factors that make schooling difficult, for example, transiency, homelessness and family responsibilities. The majority of students in flexi or second-chance schools come from such backgrounds. However, creating more of these schools may also be counter-productive in relation to moves towards a more socially just education system. The existence of such schools, for example, enables mainstream schools to abrogate their responsibilities to some of the most marginalized young people in their communities by directing 'difficult'/underperforming students to these sites. Furthermore, schools deemed to be providing students with a 'second chance' (sometimes third, fourth and fifth chances) are of many kinds and of varying quality (Raywid 1990; te Riele 2007). Some work to change the student through various behavioural programmes that treat the young person in deficit ways; some provide ready-made programmes to be delivered in standard-ized ways that take no account of the students and their backgrounds; and some work with stereotypic understandings of gender that reinscribe problematic constructions of masculinity (and sometimes femininity) (Thomson and Russell 2007). We have chosen to foreground here those sites that provide a support framework (e.g. crèches, social workers, legal support) that ensure that young people are able to attend and stay at the school, and also seek to provide the young people who do attend with a curriculum that opens up a range of post-school options for them including tertiary education.

Underpinning our project is a commitment to free public schools, but also a suggestion that they could learn much from the social justice practices and cultures evident in some alternative schools. In a study that we have recently completed for the Australian Capital Territory (Mills and McGregor 2013) we interviewed a school principal of a large government senior college that caters to year 11 and 12 students. He had been instrumental in setting up two programmes for highly disadvantaged young people, including young mothers, specifically designed to keep these young people in meaningful education. When asked about how the school addressed the 'disengagement' of students, he replied:

> I really hate the word 'disengaged'. Every time I get the chance I say to people like yourself and others that the real word is 'disenfranchised', because 'disengaged' suggests that it's the student's fault when the reality of it usually is that it's just that the education system doesn't provide anything that meets the needs of the disenfranchised.
>
> (Mills and McGregor 2013, p. 36)

We maintain that many of those young people we interviewed for this book have at some stage been 'disenfranchised', although there are clearly some who were able to avoid this by only ever having been at a school where they were included in the decision-making processes. We also suggest that many of those working in the schools represented in this book share the view of this principal and in taking up a position in an alternative school are demonstrating their opposition to a system of schooling that is oppressive for many young people. We hope that their stance and the support that they have demonstrated towards a more socially just form of educational practice will encourage debate about the future of schooling.

Appendix

Table A.1: Description of the alternative schools discussed in this book

School	Description	Location	Enrolments	Age range
Cave Street Flexi School	A very small co-educational lower secondary flexible high school, funded from donations of money from a variety of local mainstream high schools.	Open area under a suburban house that served as a youth centre, in an Australian industrial city.	21 (classes rotated in groups of 7 because of the small space).	14–16
Distincta College	A small independent, non-denominational, not-for-profit, fee-charging democratic high school. At the discretion of the principal of this school, students who could not afford the fees were permitted to attend at discounted rates. It also received some support from state and federal school funding authorities. Some bursaries and scholarships were also available.	Single heritage-listed building, in a suburb of a major Australian city.	70–80	12–18

Administrators	Teachers	Support staff (various roles)	Curriculum	Ethos
None – all such work was performed by the teacher and the youth worker.	1	1	Access 10 – this programme provides students with flexible learning opportunities to achieve an adult year 10 equivalent, relevant to their intended learning and/or training pathways.	To make young people feel welcome and safe and progress their educational goals.
1 (with teaching duties).	8	5	A strong academic programme that included Latin; Victorian Certificate of Education, and university entrance, with vocational options also available.	To encourage independent and critical thinking, personal development, creativity, self-expression and leadership qualities. Freedom.

School	Description	Location	Enrolments	Age range
Ertonia Flexible Learning Centre	An independent, non-denominational, co-educational flexible high school providing alternative pathways to young people experiencing a variety of problems in mainstream schools. Young people were referred by local high schools that funded their placements at Ertonia. Such schools are part of the 'Alternative Key Stage 4 Provision' which endeavours to avoid permanent exclusion for pupils and to encourage inclusion into education.	Located on five sites in different parts of a city in a metropolitan borough in the West Midlands of England.	Approx. 100 across four sites (some part-time). A significant number of students were dually registered at the centre and at their local high schools.	14–16
Feldspar School	A non-denominational co-educational, fee-paying independent school, operating on democratic schooling principles with strong links to the European Democratic Education Community.	A large, single building, nineteenth-century house in the south of England.	80–85	11–17
Fernvale Education Centre	A church funded single-sex high school for girls (many Indigenous) who were experiencing serious family and other personal problems, including pregnancy and motherhood. Receives some government funding.	School campus in an inner suburb of a major Australian city. It had a separate crèche just down the road from the general school.	100–110	12–25

Administrators	Teachers	Support staff (various roles)	Curriculum	Ethos
1	18	A variety of appointed mentors from referral units according to individual needs.	The school offered a range of courses that included GCSEs in core subjects such as English, mathematics, science and ICT along with preparation for work, and artistic pursuits.	To promote the rights of all young people, especially those with special (or additional) educational needs; to develop informative, understanding and supportive environments, tailored to maximize the full potential of all students.
None – the school operated on democratic principles of group decision-making.	15 plus 4 temporary/ supply teachers.	6	A range of GCSE subjects and the London Academy of Music and Dramatic Art (LAMDA) drama certificate. Personal, social and health education both as a discrete subject and through other subjects along ICT.	To promote equality, happiness and access to a good education and freedom of expression; to adhere to democratic principles of education, putting students' social and emotional development at the heart of learning.
3.5 (full time equivalent).	11 full-time (1 Indigenous) plus one part-time (0.5).	11 full-time (3 Indigenous) plus 9 part-time (5 Indigenous).	Years 8–12 Queensland Studies Authority syllabi along with a variety of vocational certificates.	To remove barriers to education and to nurture the intellectual, physical, social, emotional and spiritual development of young women: Be a peacemaker; be respectful, kind and caring, responsible and an active citizen; make a contribution; dare to be different.

School	Description	Location	Enrolments	Age range
St Ebenezer School	A non-denominational boarding and day co-educational, fee-paying independent school (kindergarten to senior high school) operating on democratic schooling principles and 100% vegetarian. St Ebenezer identified as 'multi-faith and no faith'.	A well-equipped school campus in a city situated in one of the home counties (close proximity to London) in England.	500	3–18 (for purposes of this research our interest lies with the Senior school, age range 12–18).
The Garage	A workshop that was primarily concerned with providing young people with work experience, mainly in relation to motor mechanics, charitably funded through a large community organization.	Automotive workshop situated in a low SES outer suburb of a major Australian city.	18–25	15–18 (sometimes accepted younger students).
Victoria Meadows Flexi School	A co-educational senior flexible high school, co-auspiced by a church and local government. It began in a park. Receives some government funding	A small school campus (previously closed and used occasionally as a behaviour centre for suspended students) in an inner city suburb of a major Australian city.	80–90 (40–45 full time equivalent).	15–21

Administrators	Teachers	Support staff (various roles)	Curriculum	Ethos
4 (Head, Deputy Head, Bursar and Registrar) plus 3 office staff, 4 finance officers and a Board of Governors.	Senior School 45; Junior School 14; Early Years 6; Itinerant teachers 14.	107	Montessori Early Years Programme and a Junior School plus Senior High School. For purposes of this research we were only interested in the secondary programme which has a strong academic and artistic focus for GCSEs and A Levels.	To promote mutual tolerance and respect for others and their views; to develop a community that operates on an ethos of trust and respect; to develop a local and global focus on the environment and community service.
1	3	3	Access 10 – this programme provides students with flexible learning opportunities to achieve an adult year 10 equivalent, relevant to their intended learning and/or training pathways; vocational certificates.	To provide educational, social and emotional support for the most marginalized and at-risk young people in the local area.
1.5 (full time equivalent).	4 (full time equivalent).	8	Queensland Certificate of Education, creative arts and vocational certificates; university pathways available.	To respond to the needs of young people at the margins of education; to build honest and authentic relationships with young people. This was based on the four Rs: rights, relationship, respect, responsibility.

School	Description	Location	Enrolments	Age range
West Canal Alternative School	A flexible learning centre, non-denominational, independent and co-educational, funded by local schools, County Councils, social and community services and/or parents. Donations may be received from other bodies and fundraising by the school community. It was set up to offer an alternative educational pathway to those young people who were failing to thrive in mainstream schools in the area. Approximately half to two-thirds of student referrals have statements of special educational needs.	Three separate sites in the district with its base situated in an old library in a town in a non-metropolitan county in the North West of England.	60–80 (some part-time) with classes scheduled morning or afternoon in some cases to maintain a teaching ratio of 1:6 (maximum).	13–16
Woodlands Flexi School	A co-educational flexible high school overseen by a local mainstream state-funded high school and supported by community organizations.	A large hall in a regional, medium-sized Australian city, rented from a community organization for the nominal fee of one dollar per year.	70–80	14–18

Administrators	Teachers	Support staff (various roles)	Curriculum	Ethos
1 plus an advisory board.	4	2 (plus external support services).	Curriculum modules are developed to suit the individual needs of students; Vocational qualifications, literacy, numeracy, ICTs, National Curriculum with GCSEs available depending on the abilities and prior learning of the students. Accredited adventure programme including the Duke of Edinburgh's Award (Bronze or Silver).	To create and deliver an alternative curriculum which is innovative, holistic, encourages positive progression and promotes independence. There are five principles: support, educate, encourage independence, inspire and motivate and partnership working.
1	5	3	Years 10–12 individualized pathways that provided help with literacy, numeracy and vocational studies along with the opportunity to study subjects that would lead to university entrance. This school had developed a close relationship with the local university.	To encourage young people to strive towards finding 'the greatness within'. Four common principles: respect, participation, safe and legal, honesty.

References

Australian Bureau of Statistics (ABS). 2011. *Australian social trends* (online). Available from: http://www.abs.gov.au/socialtrends (Accessed 25 April 2012).

AIG and DSF. 2007. *It's crunch time: Raising youth engagement and attainment* (online). Australian Industry Group and Dusseldorp Skills Forum. Available from: http://www.aigroup.com.au/portal/binary/com.epicentric.contentmanagement. servlet.ContentDeliveryServlet/LIVE_CONTENT/Publications/Reports/ 2007/Crunch_Time_Summary_August07.pdf.

AITSL. 2012. *Australian Teacher Performance and Development Framework* (online). Australian Teacher Performance and Development Framework. Available from: http://www.aitsl.edu.au (Accessed 6 February 2013).

AITSL. 2013. *Australian Institute for Teaching and School Leadership* (online). Available from: http://www.aitsl.edu.au/ (Accessed 1 February 2013).

Alexander, K. L., Entwisle, D. R. and Kabbani, N. S. 2001. The dropout process in life course perspective: Early risk factors at home and school. *Teachers College Record*, 103(5), 760–822.

Alsup, J. 2006. *Teacher identity discourses: Negotiating personal and professional spaces.* Mahwah, NJ: Lawrence Erlbaum Associates.

Andreas, S. 2009. *Human capital and economic growth.* Stanford, CA: Stanford Economics and Finance.

Apple, M. W. 1995. *Education and power*, 2nd ed. New York: Routledge.

Apple, M. W. 2000. Can critical pedagogies interrupt rightist policies? *Educational Theory*, 50(2), 229–254.

Apple, M. W. 2004. *Ideology and curriculum*, 3rd ed. New York: RoutledgeFalmer.

Apple, M. W. 2006. *Educating the 'right' way*, 2nd ed. New York: RoutledgeFalmer.

Apple, M. W. 2007. Whose markets, whose knowledge? In Sadovnik, A. R. (ed.), *Sociology of education: A critical reader.* New York: Routledge, 177–196.

Apple, M. W. 2010. *Global crises, social justice and education.* New York: Routledge.

Apple, M. W. 2013. *Official knowledge: Democratic education in a conservative age*, 3rd ed. New York: Routledge.

Apple, M. W. and Beane, J. A. (eds) 1999a. *Democratic schools: Lessons from the chalk face.* Buckingham: Open University Press.

Apple, M. W. and Beane, J. A. 1999b. Lessons from democratic schools. In Apple, M. W. and Beane, J. A. (eds), *Democratic schools: Lessons from the chalk face.* Buckingham: Open University Press, 118–123.

Apple, M. W. and Buras, K. (eds) 2006. *The subaltern speak: Curriculum, power, and educational struggles.* New York: Routledge.

Ashley, M. 2009. Education for freedom: The goal of Steiner/Waldorf schools. In Woods, P. A. and Woods, G. J. (eds), *Alternative education for the 21st century: Philosophies, approaches, visions*. New York: Palgrave Macmillan, 209–226.

Ball, S. J. 2003. The teacher's soul and the terrors of performativity. *Journal of Education Policy*, 18(2), 215–228.

Ball, S. J. (ed.) 2004. *The RoutledgeFalmer reader in sociology of education*. London: RoutledgeFalmer.

Ball, S. J. 2006. *Education policy and social class: The selected works of Stephen J. Ball*. Abingdon: Routledge.

Ball, S. 2012. *Global education Inc.: New policy networks and the neo-liberal imaginary*. London: Routledge.

Bardsley, K. 2007. Education for all in a global era? The social justice of Australian secondary school education in a risk society. *Journal of Education Policy*, 22(5), 493–508.

Barker, I. 2010. Swedish lesson: free schools haven't delivered diversity. *The Times Educational Supplement*, 3 December, p. 16.

Barry, M. 2005. *Youth policy and social inclusion: Critical debates with young people*. Abingdon: Routledge.

Bauman, Z. 1998. *Globalization: The human consequences*. New York: Columbia University Press.

Bauman, Z. 2004. *Wasted lives: Modernity and its outcasts*. Oxford: Polity.

Bauman, Z. 2011. *Collateral damage: Social inequalities in a global age*. Cambridge: Polity Press.

Beane, J. A. and Apple, M. W. 1999. The case for democratic schools. In Apple, M. W. and Beane, J. A. (eds), *Democratic schools: Lessons from the chalk face*. Buckingham: Open University Press, 1–29.

Beauchamp, C. and Thomas, L. 2009. Understanding teacher identity: An overview of issues in the literature and implications for teacher education. *Cambridge Journal of Education*, 39(2), 175–189.

Beck, U. 1992. *Risk society: Towards a new modernity*. London: Sage.

Beder, S., Varney, W. and Gosden, R. 2009. *This little kiddy went to market: The corporate capture of childhood*. London: Pluto Press.

Biesta, G. 2007. Education and the democratic person: Towards a political conception of democratic education. *Teachers College Record*, 10(3), 740–769.

Bjorklund, A., Clark, M., Edin, P., Fredriksson, P. and Kruger, A. 2005. *The market comes to education in Sweden*. New York: Russell Sage Foundation.

Black, R. 2011. Student participation and disadvantage: limitations in policy and practice. *Journal of Youth Studies*, 14(4), 463–474.

Blackmore, J. 2013. *Nancy Fraser and educational leadership*. London: Routledge.

Boli, J., Ramirez, F. and Meyer, J. 1985. Explaining the origins and expansion of mass education. *Comparative Education Review*, 29(2), 145–170.

Bourdieu, P. 1984. *Distinction*. London: Routledge.

British Conservative Party. 2008. *Raising the bar, closing the gap* (online). Available from: http://www.conservatives.com/Policy/Where_we_stand/Schools.aspx (Accessed 16 May 2012).

Bunar, N. 2008. The Free Schools 'riddle': Between traditional social democratic, neo-liberal and multicultural tenets. *Scandinavian Journal of Educational Research*, 52(4), 423–438.

Cabinet Office, The. 2010. *The Coalition: Our programme for government*. London: Cabinet Office.

Cameron, D. 2011. *David Cameron's education speech* (online). Available from: http://www.politics.co.uk/comment-analysis/2011/09/09/david-cameron-s-education-speech-in-full (Accessed 2 December 2012).

Carver, P. R., Lewis, L. and Tice, P. 2010. *Alternative schools and programs for public school students at risk of educational failure: 2007–08.* Washington, DC: NCES, US Department of Education.

Chilcott, T. and MacDonald, A. 2012. *Teachers plead for help with troubled students,* 11 May (online). Available from: http://www.news.com.au/national-old/teachers-plead-for-help-with-troubled-students/story-e6frfkvr-1226352499810 (Accessed 15 January 2013).

Clandinin, D. J. (ed.) 2007. *Handbook of narrative inquiry: Mapping a methodology.* Thousand Oaks, CA: Sage.

COAG. 2009. *Council of Australian Governments National Partnership on Youth Attainment and Transitions* (online). Available from: http://www.coagreformcouncil.gov.au/reports/education/national-partnership-agreement-youth-attainment-and-transitions-participation (Accessed 15 August 2013).

Cohen, J. 2010. Getting recognized: Teachers negotiating professional identities as learners through talk. *Teaching and Teacher Education,* 26, 473–481.

Connell, R. W. 1993. *Schools and social justice.* Philadelphia, PA: Temple University Press.

Connell, R. W. 1994. Poverty and Education. *Harvard Educational Review,* 64(2), 125–149.

Connell, R. W. 2009. *Gender,* 2nd ed. Cambridge: Polity Press.

Connell, R. 2011. *Confronting equality: Gender, knowledge and global change.* Crows Nest, N.S.W.: Allen & Unwin.

Connelly, R. and Clandinin, D. J. 1990. Stories of experience and narrative inquiry. *Educational Researcher,* 19(5), 2–14.

Coorey, P. 2007. Rudd vows education revolution (online). *The Sydney Morning Herald,* 23 January. Available from: http://www.smh.com.au/news/national/rudd-vows-educationrevolution/2007/01/22/1169330827940.html (Accessed 27 November 2012).

Croninger, R. and Lee, V. 2001. Social capital and dropping out of high school: Benefits to at-risk students of teachers' support and guidance. *Teachers College Record,* 103(4), 548–581.

Darling-Hammond, L. 2000. Teacher quality and student achievement: A review of state policy evidence. *Education Policy Analysis Archives,* 8(1), 1–44.

Darling-Hammond, L. 2004. Standards, accountability and school reform. *Teachers College Record,* 106(6), 1047–1085.

Darling-Hammond, L. 2010. *The flat world and education: How America's commitment to equity will determine our future.* New York: Teachers College Press.

Dawson, N. and Hosie, A. 2005. *The Education Of Pregnant Young Women And Young Mothers In England.* Bristol: University of Bristol.

Day, C. 2004. *A passion for teaching.* New York: RoutledgeFalmer.

Delpit, L. 2006. *Other people's children: Cultural conflict in the classroom.* New York: New Press.

Department for Children, Schools and Families. 2008. *Back on track: A strategy for modernising alternative provision for young people* (online). Available from: http://dera.ioe.ac.uk/7436/1/CM-7410.pdf (Accessed 15 February 2013).

Department for Education (UK) 2013. *Participation* (online). Available from: http://www.education.gov.uk/childrenandyoungpeople/youngpeople/ participation (Accessed 15 February 2013).

Department of Education, Employment and Workplace Relations. 2009. *Australian Government FactSheet: Compact with young Australians – increasing educational attainment of young people aged 15–24* (online). Available from: http://www.deewr. gov.au/Youth/YouthAttainmentandTransitions/Documents/CompactQAsWeb. pdf.

Department of Education, Training and Employment (QLD). 2011. *Pregnant and parenting students*, 2011 (online). Available from: http://education.qld.gov.au/ studentservices/inclusive/gender/pregnant.html (Accessed 15 January 2013).

Dewey, J. 1897. My pedagogic creed. *The School Journal*, LIV(3), 77–80.

Dewey, J. 1916. *Democracy and Education*. New York: Macmillan.

Dewey, J. 1938. *Experience and Education*. New York: Simon and Schuster.

DfE. 2010. *The importance of teaching. Cm. 7980*. London: The Stationery Office.

DfES. 2007. *Raising expectations: Staying in education and training post-16*. Norwich: The Stationery Office.

Dillabough, J. and Kennelly, J. 2010. *Lost youth in the global city: Class, culture and the urban imaginary*. New York and Abingdon: Routledge.

Dolfsma, W. and Soete, L. 2006. *Understanding the dynamics of a knowledge economy*. Cheltenham: Edward Elgar Publishing.

Douglass Horford, S. (ed.) 2010. *New perspectives in educational leadership: Exploring social, political, and community contexts and meaning*. New York: Peter Lang Publishing.

Dryfoos, J. 1998. Full-service schools. *Educational Leadership*, 53(7), 18–23.

Dyson, A. 2011. Full service and extended schools, disadvantage, and social justice. *Cambridge Journal of Education*, 41(2), 177–193.

Economist, The. 2011. Britain: Playground politics; Free schools. *The Economist*, 398(8720), 64.

Education Queensland. 2012. *Grounds for school disciplinary absence* (online). Available from: http://education.qld.gov.au/studentservices/behaviour/sda/ grounds.html (Accessed 5 February 2013).

Entwistle, H. 2012. *Class, culture and education*, 2nd ed. Abingdon: Routledge.

Equality and Human Rights Commission. 2010. *How fair is Britain? Equality, human rights and good relations in 2010. The first triennial review*. London: Equality and Human Rights Commission.

European Commission for Education and Training. 2001. *Second chance schools: the results of a European pilot project* (online). Available from: http://ec.europa.eu/ education/archive/2chance/repcom_en.pdf (Accessed 16 May 2012).

Evans, J., Meyer, D., Pinney, A. and Robinson, B. 2009. *Second chances: Re-engaging young people in education and training*. Ilford: Barnardo's.

Fairclough, N. 1989. *Language and power*. London: Longman.

Fielding, M. 2001. Taking education policy really seriously: four years' hard labour. In Fielding, M. (ed.), *Taking education policy really seriously: Four years' hard labour*. London: RoutledgeFalmer, 1–15.

Fielding, M. 2013. Whole school meetings and the development of radical democratic community. *Studies in Philosophy and Education*, 32(2), 123–140.

Fielding, M. and Moss, P. 2011. *Radical education and the common school: A democratic alternative*. Abingdon: Routledge.

Finlay, I., Sheridan, M., McKay, J. and Nudzor, H. 2010. Young people on the margins: In need of more choices and more chances in twenty-first century Scotland. *British Educational Research Journal*, 36(5), 851–867.

Flores, M. and Day, C. 2006. Contexts which shape and reshape new teachers' identities: A multi-perspective study. *Teaching and Teacher Education*, 22, 219–232.

Foucault, M. 1977a. *Discipline and punish*. London: Penguin.

Foucault, M. 1977b. Intellectuals and power: A conversation between Michel Foucault and Gilles Deleuze. In Bouchard, D. (ed.), *Language counter-memory, practice: Selected essays and interviews*. New York: Cornell University Press, 205–217.

Foucault, M. 1980. *Power/knowledge: Selected interviews and other writings 1972–1977*. New York: Pantheon.

Francis, B. and Mills, M. 2012a. Schools as damaging organisations: Instigating a dialogue concerning alternative models of schooling. *Pedagogy, Culture and Society*, 20(2), 251–271.

Francis, B. and Mills, M. 2012b. What would a socially just education system look like? Special Issue. *Journal of Education Policy*, 27(5), 577–585.

Fraser, N. 1997. *Justice interruptus: Critical reflections on the 'postsocialist' condition*. New York: Routledge.

Fraser, N. 2010. *Scales of justice: Reimagining political space in a globalizing world*. New York: Columbia University Press.

Fraser, K. and Chilcott, T. 2013. Classroom smackdown. *The Sunday Mail*, 13 January, pp. 1 and 4.

Fuller, B., Henne, M. and Hannum, E. 2008. *Strong states, weak schools: The benefits and dilemmas of centralized accountability*. Bingley, UK: Emerald JAI.

Gable, R. A., Bullock, L. M. and Evans, W. H. 2006. Changing perspectives on alternative schooling for children and adolescents with challenging behavior. *Preventing School Failure: Alternative Education for Children and Youth*, 51(1), 5–9.

Gale, T. and Densmore, K. 2000. *Just schooling: Explorations in the cultural politics of teaching*. Buckingham: Open University Press.

Gallagher, E. 2011. The second chance school. *International Journal of Inclusive Education*, 15(11), 445–459.

Gandin, L. A. and Apple, M. W. 2012. Can critical democracy last? Porto Alegre and the struggle over 'thick' democracy in education. *Journal of Education Policy*, 27(5), 621–639.

Giddens, A. 1991. *Modernity and self identity: Self and society in the late modern age*. Oxford: Polity Press.

Gilani, N. 2011. *Savage education cuts 'are worst since 1950s with nurseries and 16 to 19-year-olds the hardest hit'* (online). Available from: http://www.dailymail.co.uk/news/article-2053120/Education-cuts-worst-1950s-16-19-year-olds-hardest-hit.html.

Gillard, J. 2009. *Speech: Australian Financial Review – Higher Education Conference – 9 March* (online). Available from: http://ministers.deewr.gov.au/gillard/australian-financial-review-higher-education-conference-9-march-2009

Graham, L. J. 2012. Disproportionate over-representation of Indigenous students in New South Wales government special schools. *Cambridge Journal of Education*, 42(2), 163–176.

Gray, J. and Beresford, Q. 2002. Aboriginal non-attendance at school: Revisiting the debate. *Australian Educational Researcher*, 29(1), 27–42.

Green, A. 1990. *Education and State formation*. London: Macmillan.

Gvirtz, S. and Minvielle, L. 2009. Democratic schools in Latin America? Lessons learned from the experiences in Nicaragua and Brazil. In Woods, P. A. and Woods, G. J. (eds), *Alternative Education for the 21st century: Philosophies, approaches, visions*. New York: Palgrave Macmillan, 31–48.

Hall, S. 1996. Who needs identity? In Hall, S. and du Gay, P. (eds), *Questions of cultural identity*. London: Sage, 1–17.

Harber, C. 2004. *Schooling as violence: How schools harm pupils and societies*. London: RoutledgeFalmer.

Harding, J. and Pribram, E. 2004. Losing our cool? Following Williams and Grossberg on emotions. *Cultural Studies*, 18(6), 863–883.

Harper, A., Heron, M., Houghton, E., O'Donnell, S. and Sargent, C. 2011. *International Evidence on Alternative Provision (INCA Thematic Probe)*. Slough: National Foundation for Educational Research.

Hatcher, R. 2011. The Conservative–Liberal Democratic Coalition government's 'free schools' in England. *Educational Review*, 63(4), 485–503.

Hattie, J. 2003. *Teachers make a difference: What is the research evidence?* (online). Available from: http://www.acer.edu.au/workshops/documents/Teachers_Make_a_Difference_Hattie.pdf.

Hayes, D., Mills, M., Christie, P. and Lingard, B. 2006. *Teachers making a difference*. Sydney: Allen & Unwin.

Hayes, D. 2012. Re-engaging marginalised young people in Learning: the contribution of informal learning and community-based collaborations. *Journal of Educational Policy*, 27(5), 641–653.

Helbig, K. 2011. *Queensland state school suspended 320 rogue students a day in 2010, The Australian*, 30 April (online). Available from: http://www.theaustralian.com.au/news/queensland-state-school-suspended-320-rogue-students-a-day-in-2010/story-e6frg6n6-1226047234184

Hemphill, S., Toumbourou, J., Smith, R., Kendall, G., Rowland, B., Freiberg, K. and Williams, J. 2010. Are rates of school suspension higher in socially disadvantaged neighbourhoods? An Australian study. *Health Promotion Journal of Australia*, 21(1), 12–18.

Hochschild, A. 1983. *The managed heart: Commercialization of human feeling*. Berkeley, CA: University of California Press.

Huberman, M. 1993. *The lives of teachers*. London: Cassell.

Isenbarger, L. and Zembylas, M. 2006. The emotional labour of caring in teaching. *Teaching and Teacher Education*, 22, 120–134.

Keddie, A. 2012. *Educating for diversity and social justice*. New York: Routledge.

Keddie, A. 2013. Indigenous representation and alternative schooling: Prioritising an epistemology of relationality. *International Journal of Inclusive Education*. DOI: 10.1080/13603116.2012.756949

Keddie, A. and Williams, N. 2012. Mobilising spaces of agency through genealogies of race and gender: Issues of Indigeneity, marginality and schooling. *Race, Ethnicity and Education*, 15(3), 291–309.

Kilpatrick, R., McCartan, C. and McKeown, P. 2007. *Out of the box: Alternative education provision (AEP) in Northern Ireland*. Bangor: Northern Ireland Statistics & Research Agency.

Kim, J. 2011. Narrative inquiry into (re)imagining alternative schools: A case study of Kevin Gonzales. *International Journal of Qualitative Studies in Education*, 24(1), 77–96.

Kincheloe, J. 2008. *Critical pedagogy primer*, 2nd ed. New York: Peter Lang.

King Rice, J. 2003. *Teacher quality: understanding the effectiveness of teacher attributes.* Washington, DC: Economic Policy Institute.

KPMG. 2009. *Re-engaging our kids.* Melbourne: KPMG.

Kuehn, L. 2005. Control of teachers' work through surveillance. *Our Schools, Our Selves*, 14(3), 45–49.

Lamb, S., Walstab, A., Teese, R., Vickers, M. and Rumberger, R. 2004. *Staying on at school: Improving student retention in Australia.* Melbourne: Centre for Postcompulsory Education and Lifelong Learning, The University of Melbourne.

Leeder, A. and Mabbett, D. 2011. Free schools: Big society or small interests? *The Political Quarterly*, 82(S1), 133–144.

Lingard, B. 2007. Deparochializing the study of education: Globalization and the research imagination. In Gulson, K. and Symes, C. (eds), *Spacial theories of education: Policy and geography matters.* New York: Routledge, 233–250.

Lingard, B. 2009. Pedagogizing teacher professional identities. In Gerwirtz, S., Mahony, P., Hextall, I. and Cribb, A. (eds), *Changing teacher professionalism: International trends, challenges and ways forward.* Abingdon: Routledge, 81–93.

Lingard, B. 2010. Policy borrowing, policy learning: Testing times in Australian schooling. *Critical Studies in Education*, 51(2), 129–147.

Lingard, B. 2011. Policy as numbers: Accounting for educational research. *The Australian Educational Researcher*, 38(4), 355–382.

Lingard, B., Martino, W. and Mills, M. 2009. *Boys and schooling: Beyond structural reform.* Basingstoke: Palgrave Macmillan.

Lingard, B. and Sellar, S. 2013. 'Catalyst data': Perverse systemic effects of audit and accountability in Australian schooling. *Journal of Education Policy*. On iFirst: DOI:10.1080/02680939.2012.758815

Lortie, D. 1975. *Schoolteacher: A sociological study.* Chicago, IL: University of Chicago Press.

Lubienski, C. 2009. *Do quasi-markets foster innovation in education? A comparative perspective. Education Working Paper No. 25.* Paris: OECD.

Lubienski, G., Gulosino, C. and Weitzel, P. 2009. School choice and competitive incentives: Mapping the distribution of educational opportunities across local education markets. *American Journal of Education*, 115(4), 601–647.

Lucas, H. 2011. *After Summerhill: What happened to the pupils of Britain's most radical school?* Bristol: Herbert Adler Publishing.

Luke, A. 2003. After the marketplace: Evidence, social science and educational research. *Australian Educational Researcher*, 30(2), 87–107.

Lyotard, J. 1984. *The postmodern condition: A report on knowledge.* Minneapolis, MN: University of Minnesota Press.

Maguire, M. and Pratt-Adams, S. 2009. Urban primary school headship in England: An emotional perspective. *Critical Studies in Education*, 50, 1–13.

MCEETYA. 2008. *Melbourne Declaration on Educational Goals for Young Australians.* Carlton South: Ministerial Council on Education, Employment, Training and Youth Affairs.

McFadden, M. and Munns, G. 2002. Student engagement and the social relations of pedagogy. *British Journal of Sociology of Education*, 23(3), 357–366.

McGregor, G. 2009. Educating for (whose) success? Schooling in an age of neo-liberalism. *British Journal of Sociology of Education*, 30(3), 345–358.

Mills, M. 1996. 'Homophobia kills': A disruptive moment in the educational politics of legitimation. *British Journal of Sociology of Education*, 17(3), 315–326.

Mills, M. 1997. Towards a disruptive pedagogy: Creating spaces for student and teacher resistance to social injustice. *International Studies in Sociology of Education*, 7(1), 35–55.

Mills, M. and McGregor, G. 2010. *Re-engaging young people in education: Success factors in alternative schools* (online). Queensland: Youth Affairs Network of Queensland (YANQ). Available from: http://www.yanq.org.au

Mills, M. and McGregor, G. 2013. *Flexible learning options/centres in the ACT*. Canberra: The ACT Education and Training Directorate.

Mockler, N. 2011. Beyond 'what works': Understanding teacher identity as a practical and political tool. *Teachers and Teaching*, 17(5), 517–528.

Morrison, G. M. and Skiba, R. 2001. Predicting violence from school misbehavior: Promises and perils. *Psychology in the Schools*, 38(2), 173–184.

Mosen-Lowe, L. A. J., Vidovich, L. and Chapman, A. 2009. Students 'at-risk' policy: Competing social and economic discourses. *Journal of Education Policy*, 24(4), 461–476.

Munns, G., Sawyer, W. and Cole, B. (eds) 2013. *Exemplary teachers of students in poverty*. London: Routledge.

Neill, A. 1970. *Summerhill: For and against*. New York: Hart.

Newmann, F. and Associates. 1996. *Authentic achievement: Restructuring schools for intellectual quality*. San Francisco, CA: Jossey-Bass.

Noddings, N. 1996. The caring professional. In Gordon, S., Benner, P. and Noddings, N. (eds), *Caregiving: Readings in knowledge, practice, ethics and politics*. Philadelphia, PA: University of Pennsylvania Press, 160–172.

NSW DET (New South Wales Department of Education and Training). 2005. *Report of the consultation on future directions for public education and training* (online). Available from: http://www.det.nsw.edu.au/media/downloads/ reviews/futuresproject/report/z_futuresreport.pdf (Accessed 15 February 2013).

OECD. 2005. *Attracting, developing and retaining effective teachers – final report: teachers matter* (online). Available from: http://www.oecd.org/education/school/attracting developingandretrainingeffectiveteachers-homepage.htm(Accessed 1 May 2012).

OECD. 2011. *Education at a glance 2011: OECD indicators* (online). OECD Publishing. Available from: http://www.oecd.org/document/2/0,3746,en_ 2649_39263238_48634114_1_1_1_1,00.html (Accessed 25 April 2012).

Office of Public Schools, Department of Education and Training (NSW). 2013. *Aboriginal education in NSW schools. 2013* (online). Available from: https://www. det.nsw.edu.au/media/downloads/about-us/statistics-and-research/key-statistics-and-reports/aboriginal-edutraining.pdf (Accessed 16 January 2013).

Ogg, T. and Kaill, E. 2010. *A new secret garden? alternative provision, exclusion and children's rights*. London: Civitas.

Ontario Ministry of Education. 2010. *Supervised alternative learning: Policy and Implementation*. Canada: Ontario Ministry of Education.

Osgerby, B. 2004. *Youth media*. Abingdon: Routledge.

Parsons, C. 1999. *Education, Exclusions and Citizenship*. London: Routledge.

Pendergast, D. and Bahr, N. (eds) 2010. *Teaching middle years: Rethinking curriculum, pedagogy and assessment*. Crows Nest, N.S.W.: Allen & Unwin.

Perry, L. 2009. Conceptualizing education policy in democratic societies. *Educational Policy*, 23(3), 423–450.

Perryman, J. 2006. Panoptic performativity and school inspection regimes: Disciplinary mechanisms and life under special measures. *Journal of Education Policy*, 21(2), 147–161.

Pinar, W. F. 2004. *What is curriculum theory?* Mahwah, NJ: Lawrence Erlbaum.

Power, S. 2012. Redistribution, reconnaissance et représentation: parcours de la lutte contre l'injustice et des changements de politique éducative. *Education et Sociétés*, 29(1), 27–44.

Prime Minister's Office, The. 2009. *Closing the gap on Indigenous disadvantage: The challenge for Australia, 2009. An Australian Government Initiative* (online). Canberra: Commonwealth of Australia. Available from: http://www.fahcsia.gov.au/our-responsibilities/indigenous-australians/publications-articles/closing-the-gap/closing-the-gap-on-indigenous-disadvantage-the-challenge-for-australia-2009.

Queensland College of Teachers (QCT). 2006. *Professional standards for Queensland teachers* (online). Available from: http://www.qct.edu.au/Publications/ProfessionalStandards/ProfessionalStandardsForQldTeachers2006.pdf (Accessed 2 May 2012).

Quinn, M. M., Poirier, J. M., Faller, S. E., Gable, R. A. and Tonelson, S. W. 2006. An examination of school climate in effective alternative programes. *Preventing School Failure: Alternative Education for Children and Youth*, 51(1), 11–17.

Raider-Roth, M. 2005. *Trusting what you know: The high stakes of classroom relationships.* San Francisco, CA: Jossey-Bass.

Raywid, M. 1990. Alternative education: The definition problem. *Changing Schools*, 18(10), 4–5.

Raywid, M. A. 1994. Alternative schools: The state of the art. *Educational Leadership*, 52(1), 26–31.

Reay, D. 2012. What would a socially just education system look like? Saving the minnows from the pike. *Journal of Education Policy*, 27(5), 587–599.

Reid, C. 2009. Schooling responses to youth crime: Building emotional capital. *International Journal of Inclusive Education*, 13(6), 617–631.

Research and Program Development, Social Justice Unit, UCCYPF. 2011. *Uniting Care Children, Young People and Families (UCCYPF) Fact Sheet, 2011* (online). Available from: http://www.childrenyoungpeopleandfamilies.org.au/__data/assets/file/0003/60951/Suspensions_in_NSW_Schools_-_Factsheet,_UCCYPF,_February_2011.pdf (Accessed 15 August 2013).

Riddell, S. 2009. Social justice, equality and inclusion in Scottish education. *Discourse: Studies in the Cultural Politics of Education*, 30(3), 283–296.

Ritter, L. and Lampkin, S. 2012. *Community mental health.* Sudbury, MA: Jones & Bartlett Learning.

Rizvi, F. and Lingard, B. 2010. *Globalizing education policy.* London: Routledge.

Ross, S. and Gray, J. 2005. Transitions and re-engagement through second chance education. *Australian Educational Researcher*, 32(3), 103–140.

Ross-Epp, J. 1996. Schools, complicity and sources of violence. In Ross-Epp, J. and Wilkinson, A. M. (eds), *Systemic violence: How schools hurt children.* London: Falmer Press, 1–25.

Rothstein, R., Heywood, J. and Adams, S. 2009. *Teachers, performance pay, and accountability: What education should learn from other sectors.* Washington, DC: Economic Policy Institute.

Sahlberg, P. 2011. *Finnish lessons: What can the world learn from educational change in Finland?* New York: Teachers' College Press.

Sahlgren, G. 2011. Schooling for money: Swedish education reform and the role of the profit motive. *Economic Affairs*, 31(3), 1–8.

Said, E. 1994. *Representations of the intellectual: The 1993 Reith lecture*. New York: Pantheon Books.

Savelsberg, H. J. and Martin-Giles, B. M. 2008. Young people on the margins: Australian studies of social exclusion. *Journal of Youth Studies*, 11(1), 17–31.

Schools Analysis and Research Division. 2009. *Deprivation and education: The evidence on pupils in England, Foundation Stage to Key Stage 4*. London: Department for Children, Schools and Families.

Scottish Executive. 2006. *More choices, more chances: A strategy to reduce the proportion of young people not in education, employment or training in Scotland*. Edinburgh: Scottish Executive.

Scottish Government. 2008. *Closing the opportunity gap: Anti-poverty framework*. Edinburgh: Scottish Executive.

Sidorkin, A. 2002. *Learning relations*. New York: Peter Lang.

Skiba, R. J. and Peterson, R. L. 2000. School discipline at a crossroads: From zero tolerance to early response. *Exceptional Children*, 66(3), 335–346.

Slee, R. 2011. *The irregular school: Exclusion, schooling and inclusive education*. Abingdon: Routledge.

Smith, E. 2010. Underachievement, failing youth and moral panics. *Evaluation and Research in Education*, 23(1), 37–49.

Smyth, J. 2004. Social capital and the 'socially just school'. *British Journal of Sociology of Education*, 25(1), 19–33.

Smyth, J. and Fasoli, L. 2007. Climbing over the rocks in the road to student engagement and learning in a challenging high school in Australia. *Educational Research*, 49(3), 273–295.

Smyth, J. and Hattam, R. 2004. *'Dropping out', drifting off, being excluded*. New York: Peter Lang.

Smyth, J., Dow, A., Hattam, R., Reid, A. and Shacklock, G. 2000. *Teachers' work in a globalizing economy*. London: Falmer Press.

Strategic Policy and Research Program, Commission for Children and Young People and Child Guardian. 2012. *Snapshot 2012: Children and Young People in Queensland, 2012* (online). Available from: http://www.ccypcg.qld.gov.au/pdf/publications/reports/snapshot2012/education.pdf

Stronach, I. and Piper, H. 2009. The touching example of Summerhill school. In Woods, P. A. and Woods, G. J. (eds), *Alternative Education for the 21st century: Philosophies, approaches, visions*. New York: Palgrave Macmillan, 49–64.

Stronge, J. 2007. *Qualities of effective teachers*, 2nd ed. Alexandria, VA: ASCD.

Sydney Morning Herald, The. 2012. Teachers to face annual review of performance. 3 August. Available from: http://www.smh.com.au/opinion/political-news/teachers-to-face-annual-review-of-performance-20120802-23ida.html#ixzz2L8lKkhOi (Accessed 15 February 2013).

Taylor, C. 2012. *Improving alternative provision* (online). Available from: http://dera.ioe.ac.uk/13945/1/improving%20alternative%20provision.pdf.

Taylor, J. 2009. *Stories of early school leaving: Pointers for policy and practice*. Fitzroy: Brotherhood of St Laurence.

Taylor, S. and Singh, P. 2005. The logic of equity practice in 'Queensland state education'–2010. *Journal of Education Policy*, 20(6), 725–740.

te Riele, K. 2006. Youth 'at risk': Further marginalizing the marginalized? *Journal of Education Policy*, 21(2), 129–145.

te Riele, K. 2007. Educational alternatives for marginalised youth. *Australian Educational Researcher*, 34(3), 53–68.

te Riele, K. 2011. Raising educational attainment: How young people's experiences speak back to the Compact with young Australians. *Critical Studies in Education*, 52(1), 93–107.

te Riele, K. 2012. *Learning choices: A map for the future*. Melbourne: Dusseldorp Skills Forum.

Teese, R. and Polesel, J. 2003. *Undemocratic schooling: Equity and quality in mass secondary education in Australia*. Carlton: Melbourne University Press.

Thomson, P. 2002. *Schooling the Rustbelt kids: Making the difference in changing times*. Sydney: Allen & Unwin.

Thomson, P. and Russell, L. 2007. *Mapping the alternatives to permanent exclusion*. York: Joseph Rowntree Foundation.

Thomson, P. and Russell, L. 2009. Data, data everywhere – but not all the numbers that count? Mapping alternative provisions for students excluded from school. *International Journal of Inclusive Education*, 13(4), 423–438.

Thrupp, M. 1999. *Schools making a difference: Let's be realistic!* Buckingham: Open University Press.

Torres, C. A. 2009. *Education and neoliberal globalization*. New York: Routledge.

Tyack, D. and Tobin, W. 1994. The "Grammar" of Schooling: Why has it been so hard to change? *American Educational Research Journal*. 31(3), 453–479.

Unger, R. 2004. *False necessity: Anti-necessitarian social theory in the service of radical democracy*, 2nd ed. London: Verso.

US Department of Education. 2001. No Child Left Behind Act (online). Available from http://www2.ed.gov/policy/elsec/leg/esea02/index.html (Accessed 15 February 2013).

Vincent, K. and Thomson, P. 2010. 'Slappers like you don't belong in this school': The educational inclusion/exclusion of pregnant schoolgirls. *International Journal of Inclusive Education*, 14(4), 371–385.

West, M. and Peterson, P. 2003. The politics and practice of school accountability. In Peterson, P. and West, M. (eds), *No child left behind? The politics and practice of school accountability*. Washington, DC: The Brookings Institution, 620–630.

White, R. and Wyn, J. 2008. *Youth and society: Exploring the social dynamics of youth experience*, 2nd ed. South Melbourne: Oxford University Press.

White, R. and Wyn, J. 2013. *Young people and society*, 3rd ed. South Melbourne: Oxford University Press.

Williams, R. 1980. *Problems in materialism and culture: Selected essays*. London: NLB and Verso.

Williams, R. 2005. *Culture and materialism: Selected essays*. London: Verso.

Wisehart, R. 2004. Nurturing passionate teachers: Making our work transparent. *Teacher Education Quarterly*, 31(4), 45–53.

Wishart, D., Taylor, A. and Shultz, L. 2006. The construction and production of youth 'at risk'. *Journal of Education Policy*, 21(3), 291–304.

Woods, P. A. and Woods, G. J. (eds) 2009a. *Alternative education for the 21st century: Philosophies, approaches, visions*. New York: Palgrave Macmillan.

Woods, P. A. and Woods, G. J. 2009b. Introduction. In Woods, P. A. and Woods, G. J. (eds), *Alternative Education for the 21st century: Philosophies, approaches, visions.* New York: Palgrave Macmillan, 1–14.

Woods, P. A. and Woods, G. J. 2009c. Pathways to learning: Deepening reflective practice to explore democracy, connectedness, and spirituality. In Woods, P. A. and Woods, G. J. (eds), *Alternative education for the 21st century: Philosophies, approaches, visions.* New York: Palgrave Macmillan, 227–248.

Wright, E. 2010. *Envisioning real utopias.* London: Verso.

Wrigley, T., Thomson, P. and Lingard, B. (eds) 2011. *Changing schools: Alternative models making a world of difference.* London: Routledge.

Wyn, J. and Woodman, D. 2006. Generation, youth and social change in Australia. *Journal of Youth Studies*, 9(5), 495–514.

Yates, L. and Grumet, M. 2011. *World Yearbook of Education 2011: Curriculum in today's world: Configuring knowledge, identities, work and politics.* Abingdon: Routledge.

Yeatman, A. 1994. *Postmodern revisionings of the political.* New York: Routledge.

Index